# THE GUIDE FOR EVERY SCREENWRITER

## From Synopsis to Subplots: The Secrets of Screenwriting Revealed

By

*Geoffrey D. Calhoun*

Amy,

much Love!

G. Calhoun

Editor: Jayne Southern - www.southerns.eu
Cover photo and design: Adam Flor
 www.flor-creative.com

# Contents

"I read *The Guide for Every Screenwriter* in one sitting. Geoffrey D. Calhoun's book provides insight any storyteller, not just screenwriter, can use. The guide had me thinking about my script and inspired me to write within the first ten pages. What makes this book elemental for a writer is the specific simple framing of an extraordinarily complex process. Everyone has bits of their movie in their head... for those of us still learning the craft, it's easy to let a story overwhelm us and lead to failure. Geoffrey's book reaches down and provides accomplishable steps to not only get past the pitfalls, but also profoundly improve a great idea into a wonderful one."

- Pete A. Turner, Host of the Break It Down Show

"This is the book I wish I'd read ten years ago! A no nonsense, straightforward, and vital easy to follow guide for screenwriters both new and experienced. This is my new go-to guide for all things screenwriting. You better believe it'll be close by from now on."

- Cat Connor, Author of the Byte Series

"There are so many books on screenwriting. Although many of them offer tips on structure, and development, few books deliver the information into something digestible for aspiring writers. Most books can leave people feeling more confused than when they started.

The Guide for Every Screenwriter is one of the most efficient instruction manuals on the craft.

Geoffrey D. Calhoun cuts past the verbose film school expository, and gets straight to work, delivering a sample-driven checklist that anyone can follow. What's remarkable about this book is how quick it is to apply to your work. It serves as a side-by-side checklist for the writing process.

I recommend this book to anyone looking to write a screenplay, and to any professional needing a refresher."

- Kelly Schwarze, Director - Indie Film Factory

# Foreword

Like *Strunk and White's Elements of Style*, this book aims to give the reader and the writer a map to guide them. It takes the writer's hand and assists them with proper fundamentals and structure. I like this book. I like what it does if you use it properly. This miniature tome gives you the keys to the kingdom.

I've been involved with writing for over four decades. I have run over 30 Written Word Competitions over the last twenty years, read thousands of scripts, written over 300 episodes of Network Television and produced 5 films from my own screenplays (including the script for *Behind The Gate* with Academy Award Winner Joe Pesci). In short, I've seen it all. You could read one hundred books on screenwriting and still never get a tenth of the pure truth for the scribe that comes from cracking these pages open and then cracking open your mind to accept the truth of structure, process, intuition, and skill.

With this brilliant book, Calhoun has not only drawn a line, but he has also made a bulwark of design in language, style, and instruction that anyone can follow. The question is, "Will they?" I really hope they do because there are a million ways to go wrong but only a few ways to get it right. Getting it right begins with structure.

Screenwriting is one of the most difficult and rewarding crafts of all the crafts that have ever existed in the world.  Think of all the trades and skills that have died over the last two thousand years. Now consider the fact that writers have outlasted them all. Why? Because the true heroics of a story is the ability to properly format, design, create, and launch your story successfully out into the universe.

-Del Weston

This book is dedicated to:

My Muse, My Heart, and My Soul. To my wife, my son, & my mother. This one's for you.

"We are like dwarfs sitting on the shoulders of giants. We see more, and things that are more distant than they did, not because our sight is superior or because we are taller than they, but because they raise us up, and by their great stature add to ours."

**-*John Salisbury, 12<sup>th</sup>-century theologian***

# Introduction

Thank you for checking out this book! Inside we cover all aspects of screenwriting from concept to completion and what comes next. All with practical and easy to follow outlines, templates, tips, and tricks developed by a professional screenwriter.

As an autodidact, I first began my screenwriting career by tearing through books, seminars, classes, you name it. I had and still have an insatiable thirst to master this craft. I'd pester mentors until they unwillingly gave up their deepest secrets. Having done that, I was frustrated there wasn't a one-stop shop for screenwriting. I have an extensive library filled with books on the subject. Thus, I've decided to condense all of the knowledge I've gained over my ten plus years into a small, easy-to-carry guide that you can refer to whenever you need it. I will also cite several masters of the craft and their work; thus you will be able to expand your own knowledge even further.

With this book, I've compiled my slides and seminars about screenwriting into easy visuals for you to access. We will cover topics from character development, format, structure, the secrets to subplots, building your career, and everything in-between.

Please note this book is not here to discuss Aristotle, the Greek mythologies, or story structures which others have discussed prior to this work. This book refers to the modern age of screenwriting and uses popular films as examples for reference material.

I will also make you a promise. This text will not be hyperbolic and long-winded. As a screenwriter, my job is to be spartan with my writing. To use as few words as possible and make them powerful. I will not sell you fluff to impress you with my "vast knowledge." I am a working writer who has clawed his way to success over a decade of struggles. That's it. Hopefully, it will help you along your path as well. Now, let us begin.

# PART I: DEVELOPMENT

## What is Screenwriting?

Screenwriting: a visual medium conveyed through the written form. That sounds lovely and sophisticated but what does it mean? Robert Mckee in his manuscript *Story* coined the phrase "Show, don't tell." That's it in a nutshell. We show the character's journey through action and conflict.[1]

To truly understand what screenwriting is, it's best to compare it with other forms of entertainment.

### Novel:
Prose plays out through a character's ***thoughts***. Conflict is driven through their internal struggles. When you read a book, you are in a character's head and see the world through his or her eyes.

### Stage Play:
This is ***vocal***. Yes, it is on stage and we see the actors, a set, and props, but we hear a character's conflict through dialogue. Plays are all about the spoken word. Conflict is expressed verbally.

---

[1] Robert McKee, *Story: Substance, Structure, Style, and the Principles of Screenwriting,* (New York, HarperCollins), 334

*Side note:* Screenwriters like David Mamet and Aaron Sorkin are praised and hailed for their outstanding dialogue in scenes. That's because both of them were established stage writers before they shifted into screenwriting.

*The Proof:* Danny Boyle's *Steve Jobs* written by Aaron Sorkin, is a fantastic biopic feature film which has an 86% on Rotten Tomatoes, a trusted measurement of quality for Movies & TV.[2] That film is structured as a stage play, with only a few locations used repeatedly. Dialogue drives conflict the entire time. [3]

## Screenwriting:

This is *visual*. We see our character's conflict play out on screen. The best films express conflict visually and avoid the "talking heads" trap, which is excessive exposition delivered from one character to another.

*Iconic Scene:* Many hail *Citizen Kane* as the greatest film ever made. One of the best scenes is the reveal of "Rosebud" (spoiler alert). It's his childhood sled and we *see* it burning. No one talks about it. We don't hear the character's thoughts. Instead, we see that sled on fire. It is a

---

[2] *Steve Jobs* review courtesy of rottentomatoes.com.
[3] *Steve Jobs*. Directed by Danny Boyle. Universal Pictures, 2015.

visual representation of his youth, his past, and his future. All up in flames. Truly a Classic. [4]

## The "Write" Attitude for Success

Several expert writers have their own secrets to success, they have their magical "if you do this you will make it" slogan. Some people say it's luck, whereas others say it's who you know. I've studied the masters and I can tell you exactly what it takes to survive as a screenwriter and find success.

What is success? Let's tackle this for a moment. I find "make it as a screenwriter" misleading. What does that mean? The phrase itself assumes there is only one path to success as a screenwriter, which is completely untrue. Success is whatever you see it as. It's different for every writer. For some it means making serious bank, for others, it's optioning a script, others still it's joining the Writers Guild of America (WGA). It's imperative that you discover what success means to you. Then hatch a plan to manifest it. For instance, joining the WGA may prove to be a distinctly different path from making a living as a screenwriter.

There have been screenwriters who have won an Oscar for their work. Goal achieved. They never wrote another script. On the other hand, I know a writer who is too afraid to enter into competitions but whose work is brilliant. I hound them

---

[4] *Citizen Kane.* Directed by Orson Welles. RKO Radio Pictures, 1941.

constantly, but they don't care. They love to write and to them *that* is success. I wish I was as humble.

Other writers work as literary mercenaries. Shifting from gig to gig as quick as a wink while they write from the shadows, unseen and unnamed. To them, that is the life. Find what success means to you and work towards it.

Now, if success for you is being optioned, produced, or paid as a writer, then all you need are three simple things. I call them the **Three T's.**

### Time, Talent, & Tenacity

That's it. You don't need a Master's in fine arts or wild unfounded luck. Just time, talent, and tenacity. Let's break them down.

### Time

Be aware, it's going to take a while. When I say a while, I mean a decade or so. Why so long? Fair question. Malcolm Gladwell in his book *Outliers: The Story of Success* concludes that it takes 100,000 hours – approximately ten years – to truly master a craft. [5] That is a long time and a lot of hard work. But that is what it takes. There have been a few successful writers who've bucked that trend and made it early in their careers, but from

---

[5] Malcolm Gladwell, Outliers: The Story of Success, (Little, Brown and Company, 2008)

what I've observed, they are the minority. Put in the time and see what happens. Plus, do you really want your big break before you've truly mastered our craft?

## Talent

You've got to have it, or you are dead in the water. Doesn't matter how long you're willing to wait. Some believe you are either born with talent and come out of the gates really strong. Or else you are hopeless. "Too bad if you aren't a born storyteller" they'll say. I believe that is ridiculous. Talent can be cultivated. It can be learned and taught with the proper instruction and a good mentor. No one is born a blacksmith. They became one with hard work. So too does a screenwriter.

## Tenacity

Definition: "the quality of being able to grip something firmly, being very determined, persistent." This is what separates the winners from losers, my friends. This is what it's all about. No giving up. No quitting. Believing in yourself. Weathering the test of time itself is what leads you to the path of victory. It has taken me over ten years of rejections, false starts, and failed projects to see my work produced. Find the resolve within you to make your dreams happen.

## How to Write in Any Genre

"What genre do you work in?" is one of the first things you'll be asked in this industry. The expectation is that as a writer you are limited to what genre you can write in. Throughout your career, you will find people in your life who want to label you and place you in a box. Everyone from your sweet old Nana to a Hollywood producer will do it. Unfortunately, this is the norm in our industry. Many of our peers feed into this by working only on comedy or gritty grind because that's where they are comfortable. This is the wrong mindset. Versatility as a writer is what you need. The ability to push your creative muscles outside of your comfort zone will improve your writing and keep you relevant. Here's an example of why.

- *The Thomas Crown Affair* – Thriller

- *Mrs. Doubtfire* – Comedy

- *Limitless* – Sci-Fi

Three films in completely different genres. All written by Leslie Dixon: she is a powerhouse of a screenwriter who can transcend genre at will. Leslie's had a career for over 30 years in the industry.

Push yourself as a writer. Work outside of the genre you are comfortable with. Do you prefer splatter films? Then write a romcom. It will force you to become better at our craft and make you more aware of tropes and clichés you may have been missing. It's deceptively simple to write outside of your genre. But before I show you how, I have to debunk a myth first.

## Myth: "Write What You Know"

This is a great expression which is widely used and misinterpreted. People believe this statement means you should write something which is personal to you. That is only partially true. Personal stories always feel authentic because they come with an in-depth level of emotional truth, combined with details of real-life experience. However, writing what you know isn't just limited to personal stories. Anyone can write about anything if they take the time to truly learn their subject. The way to do that is through extensive ...

## Research

The internet is your friend, but books are better. Hit the local library and dive in. Read at least three books on the subject you want to write about.

## Conduct Interviews

Find experts in the topic you're writing about. This is invaluable. Sitting down with an expert and listening to them talk will not only give you plenty of great material to work with but it will also build your character. If you take the time and pay attention to your expert, you will find they have particular mannerisms and ticks, ways of speech, that you can work into a character to make them feel real.

## Outsource

There's no shame in it. Most Indie writers have a day job ... or two ... or three. You may not have the time to do the research. Hire a writer online, from a local writing group, or a college student, to ease your burden. There are even writers who start indie production companies. They hire college interns as assistants and create several low budget shorts and web series to build up their portfolios!

*Side note:* As a screenwriter, you have the Super-Power of **ALL ACCESS**. You can literally go anywhere! It's astonishing the forbidden places I've wormed my way into just by offering experts lunch and telling them I'm a screenwriter researching a movie. Doors just open for you.

## The Break Down

This is where you will watch and read at least three scripts and movies similar to the genre and style you want to write in.

- Grab a yellow legal pad.

- Take notes and pause each scene of the film.

- Write down what happens and the time marker it happens at.

  o One minute of screen time is approximately one written page of a script.

- This will teach you the flow of that genre.

- Practice this technique with at least three films.

It is a surefire way to make you fluent in a new genre and style of writing. You will have this new genre down in no time.

## Concept Development

Concept comes first. Every aspect of screenwriting relies upon this foundation. Some believe character is first. They are wrong. Character is important and is very much the soul of the story. However, without a strong concept, you end up with a snooze-fest of a script no matter how great your character is.

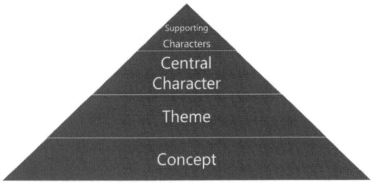

*The Script Pyramid*

The concept is the **idea** behind your script. It is the spark that ignites your creative process. A great concept can be pitched in two sentences or less.

*Example: Taxi Driver*
**Logline:** A mentally unstable veteran works as a nighttime taxi driver in New York City, where the perceived decadence and sleaze fuels his urge for violent action by attempting to liberate a presidential campaign worker and an underage prostitute.[6] [7]

There are two types of concepts the industry likes to focus on. There is the often-mentioned High Concept and the sparsely spoken of Low Concept.

---

[6]*Taxi Driver*. Directed by Martin Scorsese. Columbia Pictures Corporation, 1976.
[7] Logline courtesy of IMDb.com

## High Concept

This is a popular concept commonly talked about. There are entire seminars dedicated to revealing the secrets of how to make a high-concept film. All it is though is a concept with an easily communicable idea. It appeals to a wide audience which makes marketing less difficult. That's it. No big secrets here. Producers love a high-concept script because it has a greater chance of profitability from a wider demographic.

*Example: Jurassic Park*
Action/Adventure
Logline: During a preview tour, a theme park suffers a major power breakdown that allows its cloned dinosaur exhibits to run amok.[8] [9]

## High Concept tips

- Keep it simple

- Work on something you have a passion for

- Make it unique and atypical

- Dive into the **classics** (this works!)

- Add a **twist** to the idea

- Raise the stakes

---

[8] *Jurassic Park.* Directed by Steven Spielberg. Universal Pictures, 1993.
[9] Logline courtesy of IMDb.com

- Write about a human condition that is **universal**

- Master the genre you want to work in then break the genre to make it original

- Take a concept and push it into an entirely different direction

- Push your idea to the extreme. See how far you can take it

**Low Concept**

Also called "non-high-concept" This is the High Concept's ugly step-sibling no one likes to talk about. The focus here is on character, not plot. The character's inner emotional struggle and unique view of the world are deeply explored, i.e. a "**character study**."

*Side note*: Just because it's low doesn't mean it's bad.

*Example*: *Young Adult*
A dark comedy
Logline: Soon after her divorce, a fiction writer returns to her home in small-town Minnesota, looking to rekindle a romance with her ex-boyfriend, who is now happily married and has a newborn daughter.[10] [11]

---

[10] *Young Adult*. Directed by Jason Reitman. Paramount Pictures, 2011.
[11] Logline courtesy of IMDb.com

Types of Low Concept films:

- TV Dramas

- Indie Films

- Comedies

- Low Budget

Whether you (inevitably) decide to go with the High Concept and try to hit it big, or with a more niche-based Low Concept, always know that you need to be flexible. Sometimes as writers we tend to be a tad ... let's say fixated. We get stuck on a concept. It has to be this way or that way and we forget that we are in charge of what we write. I knew a writer who was stuck on a concept for three years. Three years! Do you know how many scripts I've written in that time?! Several of which went on to win awards, get optioned or be produced. If a concept isn't working, then set it aside. Try something else that inspires you. Come back to it later. Your mind is an exceptional problem solver. It will work on your script in the background. Return to your concept after a while and you will be astonished by the solutions you'll have. You may end up shelving the script for years, and that's okay. Just continue with your writing, and move forward on a new project. Never being stuck. That's how you break free from the pack.

## Concept Template

Answer the questions below to guide you to your next inspiring concept. These will help you define your character, the obstacles which stop them, and the genre in which you will write.

1. **Character**

   a. Who is my character?

   b. What do they need?

2. **Obstacle**

   a. Who/What stops my character from attaining their needs?

   b. How & Why it stops them.

3. **Genre**

   a. What voice do I want to use to tell this story?

   b. Does that voice make it interesting or unique?


If you get stuck and have creative challenges in answering any of these questions, then don't worry. There is a quick and easy solution for you. Simply **mind map it**.

## Mind Map

This is one of the best techniques to free you from bad cliché writing and even break out of writer's block. I've witnessed amateur writers use this and create brilliance. It is powerful and underutilized. This will allow you to access your freeform thought and make your creativity bloom.

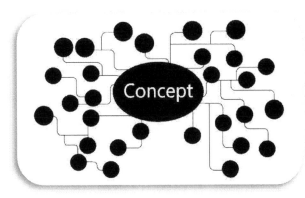

Place the question you are having trouble developing in the middle bubble then branch off. Don't be afraid to go crazy. This is your chance to truly let go and have fun. Within fifteen minutes of this exercise, you will see your concept take shape.

## Mind Map Tips

- Make it a ritual.

- Use visuals or even sounds.

- Take your time, don't rush it.

- Write down every idea.

- Do not judge your ideas.

- Be bold.

- Push your concept to the extreme.

- Don't get lost in the details.

## The Logline

A logline is a brief one-to two-sentence summary of your script. The logline is an expression of your concept and must:

- Convey the premise of your story

- Sell the idea, not tell the entire story

- Be a quick and efficient way to explain a script

- Give an emotional "hook"

- Create an interest in your script by grabbing the reader

## How to build your logline

Use the *concept template* to create your logline:

1.  Who is my Central Character?

    a.  Describe them, don't use their name, e.g., a salt of the earth mechanic, a stressed-out lawyer

2.  What does my character need?

    a.  This can be found at the beginning of Act I, i.e. Plot Point 1

3.  Who/What is stopping them?

    a.  Include what makes the Antagonist a real threat.

4.  What makes my story unique?

    a.  Make sure to hook the reader.

*Example*: *Taxi Driver*

**Logline:** A mentally unstable veteran works as a nighttime taxi driver in New York City, where the perceived decadence and sleaze fuels his urge for violent action by attempting to liberate a presidential campaign worker and an underage prostitute. [12] [13]

**Character**:
Who is our character? A mentally unstable Veteran.
What does he need? To liberate a presidential campaign worker and an underage prostitute.

**Obstacle**:
What stops him? Perceived decadence and sleaze is the real threat. This suggests he wants to save the campaign worker and prostitute from what he views as the decaying state of the city itself.

**Genre**:
What voice do I want to use to tell this story? Does that make it interesting/unique? The phrase "fuels his urge for violent action" suggests this film will be intense and vicious.

---

[12] *Taxi Driver*. Directed by Martin Scorsese. Columbia Pictures Corporation, 1976.
[13] Logline courtesy of IMDb.com

*Example: The Avengers: Infinity War*

**Logline:** The Avengers and their allies must be willing to sacrifice all in an attempt to defeat the powerful Thanos before his blitz of devastation and ruin puts an end to the universe. [14] [15]

**Character**:
Who is our character? The Avengers and their allies.
What do they need? They must defeat Thanos.

**Obstacle:**
What stops them? A blitz of devastation and ruin.

**Genre:**
What voice do I want to use to tell this story? Does that make it interesting/unique? Words like sacrifice, blitz, and end make this feel like a battle-heavy and tragic war film.

**Theme**

Whereas the concept is the idea behind the story, the *theme* is what you as the writer express to the audience. It is the **meaning** behind the idea. Theme is a must. It is not optional. Without a theme, your story will come off as flat. However, if too heavy-handed, your theme will be viewed as too preachy. **A good theme is a subtle one**. Keep coming back to the theme and make sure it

---

[14] *The Avengers: Infinity War*. Directed by Anthony Russo, Joe Russo. Marvel Studios 2018.
[15] Logline courtesy of IMDb.com

is cunningly expressed throughout the script. Consistently prove/disprove your theme throughout the story.

Some writers do not believe in developing a theme. They prefer to let the story develop "organically." Be aware, this results in the theme being whatever the writer is emotionally struggling with during the writing process.

Example: *Adaptation*
Charlie Kaufman is a gifted screenwriter having written *Being John Malkovitch, Confessions of a Dangerous Mind, and Eternal Sunshine of the Spotless Mind*. But like us he is only human and has had his struggles. Especially when he had to adapt a novel, *The Orchid Thief* by Susan Orlean. Charlie suffered from writers block and ended up writing a script about his struggles as he attempted to adapt that book. It turned into a crazy meta comedy which is brilliant all on its own and a must see for any screenwriter.[16]

Themes have *many* interpretations. Some writers use just a single word. Others write it as a sentence. Others still use a broader stroke. But, all *agree* that a theme is the moral of the story.

---

[16] Adaptation. Directed by Spike Jonze. Beverly Detroit. 2002.

## Theme Variations

- Sacrifice; Resurrection; Jealousy; Pride; Vengeance; Forgiveness; Justice; Corruption ...

- The rich can get away with murder; Faith makes life worth living; People are stronger together ...

- Coming of Age; You are your own worst enemy; Crime doesn't pay; Love conquers all ...

- (Wo)man vs. (Wo)man; (Wo)man vs.Nature; (Wo)man vs. Society ...

## Theme Template

Follow these steps to create a theme:

1. What do I want to say with my story?
   a. What is the moral of the story?
      i. Create a thematic statement.
2. How do I say it?
   a. Refine your theme and simplify it.
      i. Tie the theme to your characters arc.

## Heavy-handed vs. Weak Themes

Be careful not to get carried away with your theme, or you can end up with the story being too heavy-handed and ridiculous. This results in the story itself being overshadowed by the theme. Such as:

- *V for Vendetta* – Wage/Class disparity

- *Crash* - Racism

- *Star Wars: A Phantom Menace* – Political corruption

- *Avatar* – Exploitation of a foreign land/people

- *Click* – Choices have consequences

All of the above films had extraordinarily good concepts that suffered from heavy-handed themes, which hurt the reception of the film overall. Even *Avatar,* which was wildly successful, came under fire from critics for its overuse of theme.

Of course, there are films with hardly any theme at all. For example, many action films and horror/torture films tend to be too light on theme. Part of this is because of the genre: they rely on the visual SFX, thrilling action scenes, and shock to carry the film. Aristotle referred to this type of storytelling as "Spectacle."[17]

It was frowned upon and viewed as weak storytelling. A few examples are:

- *Transformers* – Perseverance
- *Human Centipede* – Fascism
- *The Room* – Betrayal
- *Friday the Thirteenth* - Debauchery

*Side note:* Just because it's an action film/horror, doesn't mean it has to be light on theme Example: The Matrix & Aliens have strong themes and are considered modern film classics.

## Character

Your Central Character is the soul of your story. He or she must resonate with the reader or else all is lost, and you are wasting your time. A reader starts to read your script because they like your concept. They stick around because of your characters. Your Central Character has to elicit an emotional response from the reader thus ensuring the reader is invested.

As a writer, my job is to make sure you as the reader don't go anywhere when you open my scripts. From page one, I want you to be enthralled by the story, unable to get up and

---

[17] Aristotle, *Poetics*, L. Taran and D. Goutas, (Leiden/Boston 2012)

unwilling to run for a bathroom break. The best way to do this is by making sure the Central Character is either sympathetic or empathetic.

## Sympathetic vs. Empathetic

**Sympathy** is when we understand a character's actions. It is from a more detached perspective because you may have never shared the tragedy or pain the character experiences.

**Empathy** is when we feel for a character. There is an emotional component, a deeply rooted understanding of what a character endures on their journey. This is based on the perception of a shared personal experience.

A strong and memorable Antagonist should elicit a **sympathetic** response from the reader. We need to understand why the "villain" is motivated and desperate to see their plans come to fruition. This should be grounded in the human condition. For instance, in *Avengers: Infinity War* we learn Thanos came from a world of suffering. He watched his people starve and die from over-population and lack of resources. Thus, he is dedicated to stopping this from ever happening again. We all understand the desire to never see someone suffer as we have. We just don't agree with his methods of random execution and the means by which he enacts it.[18]

---

[18] *The Avengers: Infinity War*. Directed by Anthony Russo, Joe Russo. Marvel Studios 2018

The reader must have an **empathetic** reaction to your Central Character. Sympathy alone isn't enough. We need to feel for the Central Character as they struggle on their path. This must derive from a universal human truth of emotional, physical, or spiritual pain. Something that everyone can relate to, e.g. loss of a loved one, existentialism, physical abuse, will bring a human component to your Central Character and invest the reader wholeheartedly in their journey.

*Side Note*: These two traits don't have to be mutually exclusive. Your Central Character can be sympathetic and empathetic. As can your Antagonist. In fact, the best characters are both.

## Tips on Sympathy/Empathy

- Introduce the character showing off their strengths first. What are they great at? Show it as part of the character's intro

- Establish that your character has at least one likable characteristic. Funny, lovable, geeky cute, helpful, dedicated, selfless, loyal

- Pick a trending issue from current events that are fresh and relevant such as #metoo #blacklivesmatter #stopbullying

- Use a personal struggle you are having. Break it down to its root then infuse it into your character. Write from that truth. It will give a surprising amount of depth to a character

- Give the character a yearning to change but a deep-rooted flaw that sabotages them, such as insecurity, fear, anger, depression ...

## Internal vs. External Conflict

**Internal Conflict:** the character flaw that sabotages their success. Your Central Character is constantly attempting to overcome it. The Internal Conflict is the character's inner demon, which is expressed through subtext.

**External Conflict:** the physical challenge(s) your character needs to overcome while on their path. It is the battle for survival.

Protip: The most memorable characters have a dynamic external conflict paired with an Internal Conflict which anyone can identify with, e.g., self-sabotage, loss, insecurity, loneliness, sadness ...

## Designing Your Character

Your character must have a journey that reflects the main theme. Designed from the bottom up, they need faults and weaknesses that put them on a path towards change. Your Central Character will be constantly challenged in ways that reinforce the theme of your script.

Here's a look at a few characters and how their journey reflects the main theme.

- *Jurassic Park*: The dinosaurs are breeding. Also, the family is in a fight for survival. Both of these events show the theme which is "Life finds a way"[19]

- *The Purge*: An affluent family must resort to violence when they help a stranger. This reflects the theme that no one is safe from violence. Not even the wealthy.[20]

- *The Wizard of Oz*: Dorothy is desperate to return to Kansas but can't until she truly appreciates her home.[21]

- *The Avengers Infinity War*: The theme of sacrifice appears throughout the film. Captain America fights the idea of sacrificing one's self to win the battle claiming there has to be another way. Whereas Thanos himself sacrifices the one thing he loves in the world, his daughter, to be victorious. In so doing, he forfeits his very soul.

---

[19] *Jurassic Park*. Directed by Steven Spielberg. Universal Pictures, 1993.
[20] *The Purge*. Directed by James DeMonaco. Universal Pictures. 2013
[21] *The Wizard of Oz*. Directed by Victor Fleming. Warner Bros. 1939.

## Character Sheet

Designing a character can be overwhelming. Many writers get stuck at this stage. Creating something truly special and unique from nothing should be a fun process. I grew up as a "Dungeons and Dragons" pen and paper gamer. A geek at heart, I took inspiration from a gaming character sheet and created something you can use to properly design any character in your script:

1. Name:

2. Archetype:

3. Age:

4. Ethnicity:

5. Style of dress:

6. Which child were they:

7. General outlook on life:

8. Favorite things:

9. What's in their fridge:

10. Odd quirks:

11. Worst fear:

12. What secrets do they have:

13. Lessons they need to learn:

14. Vulnerabilities – emotional/physical:

15. Past traumas:

Let's highlight a few key points:

## Name

Every name has a meaning and I infuse that into my characters for extra depth. For instance, I may name a powerful character Eric, as that name is old Norse for "Eternal Ruler."

## Archetype

From Christopher Vogler's *The Mythic Journey*: Archetypes are templates for a character's personality, i.e., a Mentor, Trickster, Shapeshifter, Shadow, all of which inform the character's traits and type of journey he or she will have. [22]

## Which child were they?

Research such as Dr. Kevin Leman's *The Birth Order Book*, suggests birth order can influence personality. For instance, the eldest child may be an overachieving perfectionist, the middle child might be a peacemaking social butterfly, and the youngest may be rebellious partiers, while an only child could be ambitious and dripping with overconfidence. This can be a fun way to layer in personality to your character.[23]

---

[22] Christopher Vogler, *The Writer's Journey: Mythic Structure for Writers,* (Michael Wiese Productions, 2008) 26

[23] Kevin Leman, *The Birth Order Book*, (Baker Publishing Group) 1998

## What's in their fridge

From Michael Tierno's book *Aristotle's Poetics for Screenwriters* which is a brilliant breakdown of Aristotle's work. In the book as a side note, Michael mentions how the inside of their fridge will tell you everything you need to know about someone. Right now, take a moment and ask yourself: "What's in my Protagonist's fridge?" It's eye-opening isn't it? Now, what's in your Antagonist's fridge? [24]

## Supporting Characters

These characters are used to reinforce the theme of the script. Subplots, either in support of or contrary to, the main theme, will help achieve this.

*Example: The Wizard of Oz*
The theme is self-discovery. Dorothy is on a journey to discover who she truly is. Is she a runaway or is she dedicated to her family? Scarecrow, Lion, and the Tin Man reinforce the theme in their quest to discover their strengths (which happen to be Dorothy's as well.) Scarecrow's plot has more focus as Dorothy finds him first, which results in him being the main supporting character with the most screen time.[25]

---

[24] Michael Tierno, *Aristotle's Poetics for Screenwriters: Storytelling Secrets from the Greatest Mind in Western Civilization*, (Hatchette Books) 2002
[25] *The Wizard of Oz*. Directed by Victor Fleming. Warner Bros. 1939.

*Example*: *Star Wars: A New Hope* The theme of "there is a hero in all of us" is reinforced by the Han Solo subplot, when Han Solo returns to save Luke Skywalker with the Millennium Falcon at the last moment of the Death Star trench run.[26]

Supporting characters also balance out the tone of a script. If a story is filled with tension and deals with a heavy topic, then a supporting character might provide comedy relief to release the tension. This works vice versa with a light-hearted film. *Example*: *The Big Lebowski*
A comedy about a man who lives a non-regimented life as an aging hippie. In contrast is Walter (John Goodman), a Vietnam war vet with anger issues so severe that he pulls a gun on a man over a bowling foul. It's brilliant writing.[27]

### *The Antagonist*
The Antagonist is more than just an obstacle for your Central Character to overcome. A great Antagonist has his/her own story arc, which runs parallel and opposite to the Protagonist's. This subplot shows the antithesis of your screenplay's main theme. The story arc reveals the inevitability of what could happen should the Protagonist fail, thus reinforcing the Protagonist's journey.

---

[26] *Star Wars: Episode IV – A New Hope*. Directed by George Lucasfilm. 1977.
[27] *The Big Lebowski*. Directed by Joel Coen and Ethan Coen. Polygram Filmed Entertainment. 1998.

*Example: Star Wars: A New Hope* Luke Skywalker's journey is that of a young moisture farmer who has no power or control in his life. He is stuck working for his grumpy Uncle Owen even though Luke desires to be a pilot. It isn't until he is forced onto an unforeseen path that he slowly comes to grips with his own power.

Darth Vader's plot, as the Antagonist, mirrors Luke's. Darth Vader is a classic villain. His subplot is about control. No one questions Vader or tells him what to do lest they suffer the invisible neck choke. This theme of control and power runs his entire arc until the end of Act III where his ship is shot by Han Solo. What happens to Darth Vader after that? He spins out of control in his damaged ship. The most powerful and feared man in the galaxy helplessly drifts away into the blackness of space. A poetic end to his arc indeed. [28]

A great Antagonist not only provides a powerful opposition to the Protagonist but also creates a lasting change in the hero. They influence the Central Character in unexpected ways which fundamentally alter the hero's internal beliefs.

---

[28] *Star Wars: Episode IV – A New Hope.* Directed by George Lucasfilm. 1977.

*Example: Black Panther*

As the Central Character, The Black Panther has lived a life of a privileged African Prince. He has never had to worry about survival aside from making sure his native land is kept safe. He believes in keeping his home of Wakanda a secret to prevent the world from taking advantage of their advanced technology and pillaging their vast resources of adamantium.

Now the film's Antagonist, Killmonger, is the antithesis of The Black Panther. He is a young black man who grew up on the streets of the inner city. He has had to fight to survive social injustices, based on the color of his skin, at every turn in his life. Crowned the King of Wakanda, he wants to use the country's influence and power to prevent another child from having to endure the pain he has lived through. He doesn't just want to open the borders of Wakanda, he wants to make it the leader of the world. He'll do so by force if necessary.

The two have a truly epic battle and Killmonger is mortally wounded. He says his piece about Wakanda and what it could be to the world. This has a surprising influence on The Black Panther and by the end of the film, he opens up Wakanda's borders to the world.[29]

Now that is a powerful Antagonist. To inflict change on another character, even after death.

---

[29] *Black Panther*. Directed by Ryan Coogler. Marvel Studios. 2018.

## Tips for Great Characters

- Make them feel real. Give the character a reason that motivates them

- A character should have an internal and external conflict

- Make your dialogue unique to each character

- Flesh out your character's traits, fears, flaws, wants and needs. From this, develop the character's subtext and inter-character relationships

- Make your character sympathetic or empathetic

- Show your character's inner emotional struggle with visual subtext

- Make the struggle something everyone can identify with

- Give the character flaws and give him/her strengths

- Discover your own hidden fears and struggles. Infuse them into your character. Writing is a form of catharsis. As your character evolves and grows, so will you

## 6 Keys to Working with a Co-Writer

Co-writing is something that every screenwriter needs to do at least once in their career. It will improve your writing by leaps and bounds. There's nothing wrong with being a lone wolf, but you miss out on the beauty of collaboration. The moment when you are in sync with a writing partner is a feeling that is difficult to describe. It's like the Tibetan proverb of explaining the taste of an orange. You can't. You have to taste the orange. It's experiential.

As with any relationship, getting to the point of *sympatico* with a fellow screenwriter can be difficult. There are plenty of horror stories out there about abandoned projects because writers couldn't work together. The secret to successful co-writing is to treat it like a partnership and not an arrangement.

### 1. Collaboration Contract

First things first, a collaboration contract must be signed. It stipulates the amount of pay, writing credits, and expected contributions both of you will make to the screenplay. This is a must. Never take a handshake. The best of friendships have been lost because of money or credit being mishandled with a project. You can download a standard contract from the WGA.

## 2. Define the relationship

Many screenwriters blindly jump into co-writing. Someone gets a great idea and brings in a co-writer without the relationship being defined. Two or three drafts later, they are at each other's throats and the project falls apart. Being passionate about a project is vital, but be smart about it. Define the working relationship between the two of you by what you expect the other writer to contribute. Is one the engine and the other a wheel? Is this a 50/50 split? Have that conversation. Yes, it will be awkward and uncomfortable, but ultimately necessary. This will help to reduce any friction should things get stressful. And they will get stressful.

## 3. Compatibility

How well you work together defines how easily the process will go. Find someone who can bring skills and talents to the table that you particularly lack or are weak in. This works two-fold. First, they will obviously balance out the script. Second, you will be able to learn from them as you work together and improve your own skills as a writer.

Constantly pushing ourselves to become better is something all of us should be doing. When I find a writer I want to collaborate with, I offer to exchange scripts and notes with them. We read each other's work and give feedback. I tell them to be honest and not hold back. You can learn a lot about a person based on how they give notes, but more importantly how they receive notes. It's a window into their soul. Are they bitter, resistant, argumentative, thankful, humble, or gracious? This will tell you if you can work with them or not.

## 4. Trust & Respect

Without trust and respect, there is no partnership. They are the foundation of a solid collaboration. After we give each other notes and have decided we are compatible, I go one step further. I get to know them through several "creative" meetings on story development. Once we feel comfortable with each other, then I know that trust is building and it's time to move forward with the project. You might ask, "How do you know when trust is building?" Simple, are they comfortable sharing things about themselves with you? Do you look forward to seeing or talking with them? And most importantly, do they make you laugh? If the answer to these questions is yes, then you are starting to build trust.

Respect for your co-writer's skill as a writer is a given. You wouldn't be collaborating with them if you didn't respect what they can do. It's about respecting their creative vision and keeping their "voice" in the script. This is something to keep in mind during the rewrite. Especially, when it comes down to cleaning up the script and making it seem like "one person" wrote it.

How do you make two separate writers come across as one? You do a draft together where you both comb through the script side by side and make it as clean and lean as possible. Eventually, if you work with this person enough, you both will write in a way that is almost indecipherable from one another. It will be as if one person is writing. That is when you hit that beautiful moment of *sympatico*.

## 5. Set the ego aside

The work is what matters most. Not you or your ideas. The script. You can't become too attached to an idea. This unfairly limits the contributions of your co-writer. You must remain open. If you spend most of your sessions arguing with your writing partner about the story, then I've got news for you: you're the problem. You need to step back emotionally from the work. Listen to what they have to say. It's okay to disagree with them, but make sure you have a compelling reason why it should go your way. Usually, the best solution is something neither of you has thought of yet.

However, sometimes you hit an impasse. That's when it's a good idea to have a "trade-off" rule. If there is a moment in the script in which you must have the scene exactly as you envision it. Your co-writer has to respect the trade-off and allow it. Now they are free to make a single change which they want as well. Of course, the trade-off should be used sparingly on a script. Don't abuse it.

## 6. Figure out your style

There are myriad ways to co-write a script. Some will pass scripts back and forth. Others will break up which scenes, acts, or even characters each writer will exclusively write. There have even been teams where one co-writer will dictate as the other types. Always do your outline together as a team. No exceptions! I prefer to write the entire script side by side with my co-writers. I feel it's the best way. You have each other, right there, and can constantly try out what works and what doesn't in the moment.

There you have it, the fundamentals of developing a script from concept to collaboration. This part of the process can be daunting with its own unique successes and failures. But, we're writers after all, and are made of the strongest stuff in the world. Persistence.

Patience, however, is the true cornerstone of this process. Never be afraid to take a step back for a wider perspective on the story. It's too easy to get lost in a cone of focus when zeroing in on it with noses buried in keyboards.

# PART II: STRUCTURE

Structure is simply the way your script is organized to create a dynamic story of events and conflict which unfold during your characters' journey. I say "simply," but it is actually deceptively simple. Which is why it can be so difficult to tackle when writing.

Several masters have created their own systems of structure going all the way back to Joseph Campbell's *The Hero with a Thousand Faces*. In this text he revealed the monomyth which details specific trials and challenges a protagonist must encounter while on their journey. [30]

Christopher Vogler famously explored and adapted Campbell's work into his popular book *The Writer's Journey*, which made it even more widespread as Vogler brought the monomyth to Disney. Thus, the Disney films are so powerful yet ultimately similar in their storytelling. [31]

Blake Snyder further broke down the monomyth with his popular book *Save the Cat*, which has been very well received over the years. Several other systems of writing structure have popped up since. What these systems have done, knowingly

---

[30] Joseph Campbell, *The Hero with a Thousand Faces*, (New World Library, 2008) 29
[31] Vogler, *The Writer's Journey*

or not, is to pick certain parts of monomyth and call it their own. [32]

Out of all of these systems, the easiest way to understand basic structure is through Syd Field's Three-Act Paradigm from his book *Screenplay*. It is the most pared-down form of structure to date. [33]

Now originally this three-act structure was designed for a 120-page script. No one writes scripts that long anymore. Thus, I have updated his structure to accommodate a ninety-page script which is more in line with current standards of screenwriting. A story can be easily divided into three sections:

## Syd Field's Three-Act Paradigm

1-25 pages    25-65 pages    65-90 pages

---

[32] Blake Snyder, *Save the Cat: The Last Book on Screenwriting You'll Ever Need*, (Michael Wiese Productions, 2005)
[33] Syd Field, *Screenplay: The Foundations of Screenwriting*, (Bantam Dell, 2005)

**Act I -** Setup: (Beginning) This shows the main character and the world they live in. This is life as it is normally. We set up for the story to change. We show who the characters are, their strengths and weaknesses, and why the reader should be invested in them.

**Act II** - Confrontation: (Middle) This describes the confrontations and challenges the main character has to encounter. Our character will continue to fail these ever increasingly difficult challenges until he/she realizes they have to adapt and change in order to succeed.

**Act III** - Resolution: (End) By this point the hero has adapted and changed significantly. He or she now has the tools to successfully confront the enemy. This results in a definitive victory.

The three-act structure is an important first step. Syd Field builds it out even further with his *plot points* and what he termed as *pinches*. These are essential as well, but the structure needs extending just a little further to allow for a creative vision to prosper.

Thus, I've built upon Syd Fields system and pooled in a few extra bits and pieces to create a nine-point structure. I don't believe in reinventing the wheel. What I do believe in is efficiency. As screenwriters, we need to be able to write quickly. I've had gigs come down the pipe that needed a twenty-four-hour turnaround because shooting was to start the next day. With a project like that, a writer can't be bogged down by an overly sophisticated system. There are other outlines available as well, but I find them too formulaic and creatively oppressive.

By amalgamating advice from the greats, this outline allows a screenwriter the freedom needed to express creativity and originality while still providing a focused structure. Especially if a writer has to burn the midnight oil.

## Nine Point-Main Plot Outline

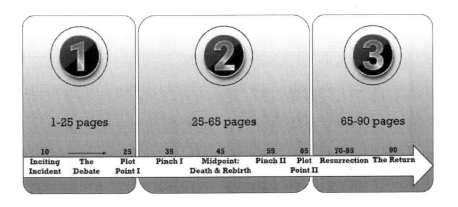

Also called story "beats," these are the set trials and moments in the script which the Central Character must experience throughout the story.

## Act One

**Inciting Incident: (**Page 10) Sets the story in motion. It draws the Central Character into the main plot and is a universal moment found in all structure methods.[34]

**The Debate:** Drawn from Blake Snyder's *Save the Cat*. This is an important moment in our characters' journey. They hem and haw over being called to action. It shows how we as people fight change. When we show our characters do that as well, it makes them more human and gives us empathy for them.[35]

**Plot Point 1:** (Page 25) The true beginning of your story. It is a moment of conflict which progress the story into Act II.[36]

## Act Two

**Pinch 1**: (Page 35) A sequence which focuses on the central conflict and ushers the story forward. In *The Wizard of Oz*, this is where Dorothy discovers and helps her new traveling companions.[37]

**Midpoint: Death & Return:** (Page 45) A significant event which causes the Central Character to experience a spiritual, intellectual, emotional, or even physical death. The character

---

[34] Field, *Screenplay*
[35] Snyder, *Save the Cat*
[36] Field, *Screenplay*
[37] Syd Field, *The Screenwriter's Workbook*, (Bantam Dell, 2006)

has no choice in the matter. The Central Character has to lick his/her wounds and pull him/herself up by the bootstraps to carry on. This moment tends to have a further revelation which can alter the direction of the story.

**Pinch 2**: (Page 55) Reflects Pinch 1. Reveals what emotional/physical challenges the Central Character has yet to defeat.[38]

**Plot Point 2**: (Page 65) An event that is the *point of no return* for the Central Character, also referred to as the "Reward" by Campbell's work. This is a new weapon, strength, or knowledge the Central Character discovers. This moment fully commits the hero to the story as they are ready for the final battle.[39]

Act Three

**The Resurrection:** (Page 70-85) From Vogler's *The Writer's Journey*. The hero has newfound knowledge and strength gained from Plot Point 2. This is a second death and rebirth moment during the final battle or climax. The difference between this and the midpoint of Act II is a matter of choice. During the midpoint, a death and rebirth are thrust upon the Central Character. She/he has no choice in the matter. Whereas during the resurrection, the Central Character chooses to

---

[38] Syd Field, *The Screenwriter's Workbook*
[39] Field, *Screenplay*

sacrifice her/himself for the greater good, love, friendship, et al.[40]

This choice is what cements their journey. This is the moment in *The Matrix* when Neo chooses not to run and accepts himself for who he truly is. Instead he chooses to fight agent Smith. A decision he knows will lead to his inevitable death.[41]

**The Return:** (Page 90) In *Hero with a Thousand Faces* Campbell states the hero must return to the people with his gifts. This is the final segment in the story and is the resolution of the main plot and the event from Plot Point 2. This must end in an emotionally satisfying way. [42]

To quote David Mamet, "... tell a magnificent story and tell it in a way that the ending is surprising and inevitable ..."[43]

In *The Wizard of Oz*, it is Dorothy, as she awakens in bed with a newfound love and appreciation for family and friends.[44] In *The Matrix,* it is Neo's final monologue giving a warning to the Matrix, then surprisingly flying away.[45]

[40] Vogler, *The Writer's Journey*
[41] *The Matrix*. Lana Wachowski and Lilly Wachowski. Warner Bros. 1999.
[42] Campbell, *The Hero with a Thousand Faces*
[43] David Mamet, Masterclass.com
[44] *The Wizard of Oz*. Directed by Victor Fleming. Warner Bros. 1939.
[45] *The Matrix*. Lana Wachowski and Lilly Wachowski. Warner Bros. 1999.

## Beyond the Nine

A nine-point outline is lean and allows for plenty of creativity. It can also be easily built upon. For instance, each point or "beat" of the nine-point outline can be broken down into three scenes. That is 27 scenes total per script. That's it. Each scene should be no more than three pages. Anything longer bogs the screenplay down and causes the reader to lose interest.

```
              ┌── Page
        Scene ┼── Page
       /      └── Page
      /       ┌── Page
Beat ─── Scene┼── Page
      \       └── Page
       \      ┌── Page
        Scene ┼── Page
              └── Page
```

With 27 scenes at three pages each, your script will come in at 81 pages, which leaves a nice amount of creative wiggle room for you to play with. Remember, a good script length is from 86-106 pages.

A great way to create scenes around the nine-point outline is to utilize a part of the structure which tends to be severely underdeveloped in most scripts.

We are talking about...

## Subplots

As a professional screenwriter and script consultant, I receive many scripts to repair. More often than not these feature-length scripts are short on content. They usually run from 60-70 pages and the writers/producers don't know why they're so short. The answer is simple. Subplots. The main plot can only take you so far. You need subplots to add content and buff out your story.

That being said, don't just fill your script with random subplots to hit your page mark. That creates an erratic story which will be lambasted by the film community. It's best to use subplots which either support your main theme or express the antithesis of it.

Robert Mckee said it best in his book *Story*. He states, *"Subplots may be used to resonate with the controlling idea of the central plot and enrich the film with variations on a theme."*[46]

Here are the subplots you can use to properly develop your script, characters, and their interrelationships. All while reinforcing the main theme of your script. They are:

- Subplot 1 (The Heart Plot)
- Subplot 2 (A Supporting Character)
- Subplot 3 (The Antagonist)

---

[46] McKee, *Story* 227

These subplots intersect with the Central Character's main plot at key points. Weaving these together creates a fulfilling and well-developed script which is exciting to read.

## Subplot 1 - The Heart Plot

This is the emotional hook of the story. Also referred to as the "B" plot. It is often reduced to the love interest or romance plot, but that is only one use of the heart plot. This plot should create an emotional depth to the script. It allows a glimpse into what makes the Central Character human.

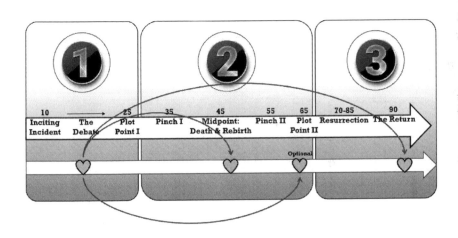

For instance, the heart plot can be centered between Mentor and Student, as it is for Obi-Wan and Luke. It can be a mix of multiple archetypes into a complex love arc, as it is between Jackson Maine and Ally from *A Star is Born,* or the obscure, such as *John Wick* and his dog which is a representation of his deceased wife's love.[47]

**The Debate:** This is the intro to the heart aspect of our story. It is the "follow the white rabbit" scene where Neo meets Trinity in *The Matrix*.[48] Or when Jackson Maine discovers Ally and wants to take her on tour with him in *A Star is Born*.[49] In a romantic heart plot, this is also called the "meet cute" scene.

**Midpoint**: The Heart Plot has a big crescendo here as it is directly related to death and rebirth. This is where Obi-Wan is killed in *Star Wars: A New Hope* which leaves Luke at his lowest.[50] Or when Dorothy is put to sleep by the evil Wicked Witch of the West in *The Wizard of Oz*.[51] In a romantic plot, it is the big break-up scene. In a buddy comedy, it is the falling out of favor moment.

---

[47] *John Wick*. Directed by Chad Stahelski. Thunder Road Pictures. 2014.
[48] *The Matrix*. Lana Wachowski and Lilly Wachowski. Warner Bros. 1999.
[49] *A Star is Born*. Directed by Bradley Cooper. Warner bros. 2018.
[50] *Star Wars: Episode IV – A New Hope*. Directed by George Lucas. Lucasfilm. 1977.
[51] *The Wizard of Oz*. Directed by Victor Fleming. Warner Bros. 1939.

**Plot Point II:** This is optional. As the Central Character is still recovering from the midpoint, they can turn to the heart plot to find strength. This is a moment Vogler refers to as the "Reward" where the Central Character finally finds inner strength. In Star Wars: *A New Hope,* Luke is dealing with the loss of his Mentor and he is supported by Leia. For *John Wick*, it is when he discovers the new dog.[52]

**The Return:** The ultimate conclusion of the heart plot. It reflects how the Central Character has changed for better or worse. This can be the final kiss; the "you had me at hello"[53] moment from *Jerry Maguire*; a literal reward such as the medal given to Luke Skywalker; or as in Young Adult when the Central Character, Mavis chooses to walk away from love, and resume her life as a selfish person.[54]

## Subplot 2: The Supporting Character

This focuses on a supporting character. It is used to subtly call back to the theme, and either the thesis or antithesis of the story. It can show a possible positive or negative outcome for the main plot, or used as a cautionary tale of what can happen to the Central Character. or as a hint of positivity that is to come at the end of the Central Character's journey.

---

[52]*John Wick*. Directed by Chad Stahelski. Thunder Road Pictures. 2014.
[53] *Jerry Maguire*. Directed by Cameron Crowe. Tristar Pictures, 1996.
[54] Young Adult. Directed by Jason Reitman. Paramount Pictures. 2011.

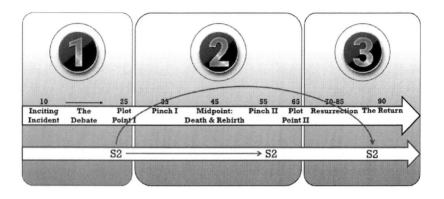

**Plot Point:** Here the supporting character is introduced, typically in a moment which reveals his/her character in a way that paints them as unique. The supporting character should not blend with your Central Character. He/she needs to stand out, yet not outshine the hero. In *Star Wars: A New Hope,* Han Solo is introduced in the Cantina where he is in negotiations with Luke and Obi-Wan.[55] Han makes it very clear he's in it for the money. Shortly after, Han unceremoniously murders a bounty hunter who is after him (Han shot first!) This reveals his character. He is a scoundrel, not an innocent young boy, as is the hero Luke Skywalker.

---

[55] *Star Wars: Episode IV – A New Hope*. Directed by George Lucas. Lucasfilm. 1977.

**Pinch II:** Here the supporting character is presented with an opportunity to change. To show how much he/she has grown during the journey. This is very much the midpoint: death and rebirth of the supporting character. He/she will fail this test and revert to his/her old ways, instilling doubt that even the Central Character may fail as well. This is when Luke asks Han Solo to join him on the Death Star attack run but Han declines as he is only in it for the money.[56]

**The Return:** During the climax and final battle our supporting character will realize the change he/she needs to make and will appear to assist the Central Character on their journey in some way. This is when the Millennium Falcon swoops in to save Luke from Darth Vader's Tie Fighter. This is the moment Ally returns to Jackson Maine's side when he is released from rehab. She is willing to give up everything to ensure his sobriety.[57]

## Subplot 3: The Antagonist

This is the development of the Antagonist as a character who is worthy of taking on the Central Character. His/her plot should run alongside, and diametrically oppose, the main plot. This subplot is not limited to the Antagonist as a character. It can also be used in (wo)man vs. nature scripts as

---

[56] *Star Wars: Episode IV – A New Hope.* Directed by George Lucas. Lucasfilm. 1977.
[57] *Star Wars: Episode IV – A New Hope.* Directed by George Lucas. Lucasfilm. 1977.

well. Each plot should show the progression of the "disaster" and its effects on our characters.

There is scope for even more creativity with the Antagonist, such as in *A Star is Born*. The Central Character is Jackson Maine and the Antagonist is his addiction. He is his own worst enemy. As the story progresses, his addiction worsens as he battles himself for survival.[58]

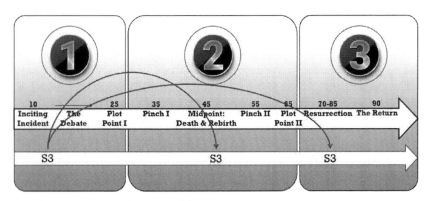

The more closely bound the Central Character and Antagonist plots and themes are, the more powerful your story will become.

Let's dissect Darth Vader's plot in *A New Hope*. At first glance, he seems like a shallow prototypical villain: black ensemble and a cape sans the goatee. But look deeper and you will see a subplot staring you in the face the entire time. That plot is ... control/power.[59]

---

[58] *A Star is Born*. Directed by Bradley Cooper. Warner bros. 2018.
[59] *Star Wars: Episode IV – A New Hope*. Directed by George Lucas. Lucasfilm. 1977.

**Inciting Incident:** The Antagonist's plot begins either before or soon after the Inciting Incident. Either is fine as long as it is tied to the event. In *The Wizard of Oz*, Ms. Gulch (the Wicked Witch) arrives at Dorothy's house with an order to have Toto euthanized. This drives Dorothy to take her dog on the run which inevitably leads Dorothy to Oz. This moment also sets off the Wicked Witch's plotline to try to destroy Dorothy and Toto.[60]

**Midpoint:** This is where the Antagonist receives a large dose of development. We learn his/her true motivations as her/his plans are revealed and the Protagonist is at her/his mercy.
At this point in the journey, the Antagonist is at his/her most powerful while the Protagonist is at her/his weakest.

Darth Vader is the most feared person in the galaxy and that is shown early on. We learn this when he single-handedly chokes a rebel soldier. But we soon learn he also likes to be in total control. Thus he will not tolerate being questioned and force chokes a general in front of his peers. This Arc of Control follows throughout the entire story. He even allows the rebels (Luke, Han, and Obi-Wan) to escape.[61]

---

[60] *The Wizard of Oz*. Directed by Victor Fleming. Warner Bros. 1939.
[61] *Star Wars: Episode IV – A New Hope*. Directed by George Lucas. Lucasfilm. 1977.

In *The Wizard of Oz*, we learn it's all about the slippers. If the witch possesses them, she will be the most powerful being in the land and unstoppable. Being able to avenge her sister's death at Dorothy's hand will be an added bonus.[62]

**Resurrection:** This plot finishes at the hero's resurrection, which is the ultimate death of the Antagonist. Thus, there is balance. Here the Antagonist's plot is complete, and we see the natural end of his/her path. For Darth Vader, he is in total control until his Tie Fighter is shot by Han Solo. Then his ship careens off course and what happens to it? It spins out of control. He is helpless. Whereas Luke has discovered his inner power, Darth Vader has lost his.[63]

*Side Note*: The above three plot points are where the Antagonist truly intersects with the main plot. As the arc suggests, several more subplots may intersect at any time in the script. This is an excellent way to build the Antagonist and keep the story going forward. Is the main plot sagging? Bring in the Antagonist and watch the pace quicken. This works.

[62] *The Wizard of Oz*. Directed by Victor Fleming. Warner Bros. 1939.
[63] *Star Wars: Episode IV – A New Hope*. Directed by George Lucas. Lucasfilm. 1977.

# Main plot & Subplot Arcs Combined

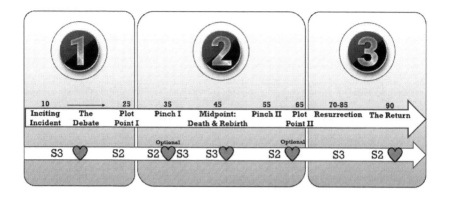

**Pinch I:** This is the first real trial of the Central Character. As such, you can place any part of the subplots here accordingly. It just depends on what you want to develop more. You can even use all three. In *A New Hope*, all three were used as the Empire blows up Alderaan in front of Princess Leia. This then led into the heart plot of Luke and Obi-Wan recovering from a "disturbance in the force" Han's plot is also developed in this scene when he mentions he doesn't believe in hokey religions. A blaster at his side is all he needs, which reveals the only thing he trusts in the galaxy is himself.[64]

---

[64] *Star Wars: Episode IV – A New Hope*. Directed by George Lucas. Lucasfilm. 1977.

## Structure Tips

- Avoid "talking heads." Give characters something to do while in dialogue

- Remember, your subplots need to reflect the main plot

- Pacing is key. Every scene must move the story forward while increasing tension

- Create interest in every scene with twists, surprises, and misleads

- Take exposition out of the dialogue.

- Don't have conflict for the sake of conflict. It must serve the story or the character's journey

- Avoid solving plot holes via random chance aka Deus Ex Machina!

# PART III: FORMAT

Screenwriting is written in a specific way which is unique and different from any other literary work. This is called formatting. It is an industry standard which is expected in a screenplay. There is no wiggle room. Even the font is a particular type and size: Twelve point, New Courier is the standard. It was created to mimic the old typewriter fonts screenplays used to be written with.

Formatting a script to perfection separates you from an amateur. It is just one way to edge your script ahead of the others. If a producer/studio reads a script which is improperly formatted, there is only one destination for it. The trash.

Formatting is incredibly difficult to learn. It is like learning a whole new language and way for a writer. Let's look at the basics.

## Reading vs. Shooting Script

This book will focus on techniques for a reading script. A *reading script* is one that is meant to be pleasing to the eye. It is what producers and studios expect from a screenwriter when they receive a screenplay. The camera directions are kept to a minimum. A *shooting script* is the opposite and typically done by the Director. This script is heavy on camera directions as it is the draft used for production.

## Passive vs. Active Speech

A script must be written with an active voice such as she swims, she runs, she types. Verbs should never appear passive, such as: she's swimming, she's running, or she's typing.

**The Title Page:** Clean and simple. No crazy pictures on top. Keep the title standard. No need for fun, flashy, or colorful, typeface as that screams amateur. The WGA /Copyright doesn't need to be included on the draft as it will be requested at a future date if the producer is interested. Do include your contact info.

*No pictures

Standard fonts

A MIGHTY QUEST

By

Geoffrey D. Calhoun

*No WGA registration # or Copyright needed on the title page

info@wefixyourscript.com ←——— Contact info
601-885-3491

## Basic Formatting

**Fade in:** This is a transition. It is used before we begin the script and also comes in again at the very end of the screenplay as either:

FADE OUT or FADE TO BLACK.

**Primary Scene Header:** Aka the Slug line. This is the location of the scene. It begins either with EXT. for exterior or INT. for interior. Followed by where the scene is, for example, the APARTMENT BUILDING COURTYARD and is finished by either DAY or NIGHT, depending on when the scene takes place.

**Action:** This is a brief description of what happens in the scene. The key word here is "brief." Keep it to four lines. Leave superfluous description to the novelists. Screenwriting is about the economy of words: less is more but make them powerful. Use active speech not passive. Use she swims, walks, talks instead of she is swimming, talking, or walking. Read the very first action line in the example on the following page and see how it paints a picture of the scene with only two lines.

**Character Intro:** Used only for the first appearance of a character with dialogue. Capitalize the name and add a brief description. This description needs to capture the essence of who they are. Do not focus on their looks.

*Primary Scene Header*

*Must have* ⟶ FADE IN:

EXT. APARTMENT BUILDING COURTYARD - DAY

The tall, brick apartment building reaches high into the sky like a medieval tower.

*Character intro* ⟶ JONAH, a sweet 10-year-old boy, sits alone at a weathered picnic table.

EXT. PICNIC TABLE BATTLEFIELD - DAY

A great toy battle has been fought on this table.

*Action:*
*No more than* ⟶ There's a greasy ogre tipped over on it's side, a set of
*four lines* dominoes stacked like an ivory staircase, and a tiny, beat-up plastic action figure of SIR GAWAIN, a brave knight in gray armor, who stands tall and proud.

                    JONAH (O.S.)
                 (as Sir Gawain)
        Let her go, Baron Von Naughty.

**Secondary Scene Header:** This is used when a character is in a location and moves into another room or somewhere nearby. It makes the script more efficient and reads faster. Below is an example.

INT. APARTMENT BUILDING LOBBY - DAY

Jonah enters the old lobby. The walls are damaged and the tile floors are cracked. There is hardly anyone there.

The building MANAGER, a tall and massive Neanderthal-looking fellow in his 50s, naps behind the front counter.

FRONT COUNTER ⟵ *A Secondary Scene Header can be used when we see a character move between scenes*

Jonah sneakily walks around the corner and creeps up to him.

A large ring of keys hang from the Manager's hip.

Jonah looks about left and right. No one can see him. With deft hands, Jonah grabs the keys and gives them a tug.

65

Since Jonah never left the apartment building lobby and merely moved to the front counter, we can skip the extra description and use FRONT COUNTER. If a character moves to a completely different location, then a secondary header becomes confusing and is to be avoided. However, if a character is in a home and is moving between rooms, then a secondary header is perfect to use.

**Parenthetical:** Aka the Wryly. This is used to provide the actor with a specific way to read the dialogue. This needs to be used sparingly and is only used if the dialogue or action doesn't insinuate the way the line should be read.

```
INT. DAISY'S APARTMENT - FAMILY ROOM - DAY

Jonah quietly locks the door. On a nearby couch stirs Daisy's
father BARRY, a grease monkey in his late 30s. Still asleep,
Barry rolls over to reveal a silly logo of a car and taco on
his shirt which reads "Barry's Autos and Tacos."

Jonah snickers at the logo then quickly hides behind a chair.

Jonah crawls towards Daisy's room. He comes to a stop when a
large, black dog greets him with a growl. From its thick neck
hangs a name tag that reads "Drake".

                        JONAH
                  (fearful)  ←——— Parenthetical
            The Black Dragon.

Drake slowly pushes towards Jonah; its jowls full of slobber.
The mutts beady eyes stare him down as if he's a fresh dinner
to be devoured.
```

*Side note:* Wryly is a word which was so overly used that it has become synonymous with parentheticals themselves. That being said, never use the word wryly in your script as it will demean your work.

**O.S.** stands for off-screen in moments when a character is present but not seen during dialogue.

```
EXT. PICNIC TABLE BATTLEFIELD - DAY

The knight stands tall as a few cookie crumbs, which appear
like boulders, crash down nearby with earth-shattering BOOMS.

                    JONAH (O.S.) ←———  Used for off screen dialogue. If
                 (as Sir Gawain)       the character is not present in
              Your magic cannot stop me.  the scene use V.O.
```

**Flashback:** Used to call back to an early moment in the script or event which is somehow related to the overall story. If there is a particular set year which is important to the story, then you can use that in place of flashback.

```
INT. HOSPITAL - DAY - FLASHBACK ←——  Flashback begins here

Jonah lays in a hospital bed, pale and weak, with an oxygen
mask over his face. His PARENTS are behind a curtain with a
DOCTOR, washed out by a white light.

                    MOTHER (O.S.)
              What are you saying?

                    DOCTOR (O.S.)
              He needs to be careful. Too much
              exertion will take its toll. He got
              lucky this time.

INT. APARTMENT STAIRCASE - PRESENT DAY ←——  Marks the end of the
                                            Flashback
The manager catches his breath.
```

**Quick Flash:** This is when a sudden "flash" of an image(s) appears on the screen. A quick flash is a versatile technique which can be used for a dramatic revelation of plot or to create a build-up of tension within a character. Use them sparingly. Too many will numb the reader at best or confuse them at worst.

```
QUICK FLASH - JONAH AND DAISY MEET IN THE HOSPITAL  ←─ Quick Flash
                                                        begins here
-- Jonah is pushed in a wheelchair by his mother. Jonah sadly
contemplates the inhaler in his hand.

-- Daisy passes Jonah as she walks with her father. She
appears healthy.

-- Jonah turns around, as does Daisy. They lock eyes. Jonah
smiles to her. Daisy shyly smiles back and waves.

BACK TO SCENE  ←── Quick Flash ends as the previous scene continues

Jonah notices how upset Daisy is. He sits down on the bed
next to her. He gently reaches out to her face. She shies
away. He delicately removes her wig and sets it aside.
```

## Phone Conversations:

There are several ways to do these. The easiest is to have a one-way conversation where a character's dialogue is one-sided and we never hear what is said at the end of the line. When done well, this adds an element of tension and mystery as the reader/audience is in the dark on the conversation. At worst it reads as lazy writing, so use this technique carefully. Other ways to write a phone conversation are:

**V.O. (voice-over):** with this you can have the other character heard over the phone. You must use the *filter* parenthetical, so the reader knows the character's voice sounds as though it's over the phone. V.O. can also be used as narration from a character who is not onscreen. Such as in the opening exposition in *Lord of the Rings*.

**Intercut:** The final way you can present a conversation is by *intercutting* the scenes. This uses a new scene header which allows the camera to cut between speaking characters. On the following page is a scene which illustrates all three techniques for phone conversations.

```
EXT. JONAH - DAY

Jonah looks up and sees Daisy is gone. Only an empty and open
window remains.

                    JONAH (O.S.)
                (as Sir Gawain)
            Fear not, princess. I will free you
            and smite this foul --

The sound of SWORDS CLASHING rings through the air. This is
Jonah's ringtone. He whips out his cell phone.

His eyes narrow with caution as a picture of Lady Guinevere
blinks on the phone. The screen reads "Mom."

Jonah answers the phone.

                    JONAH
            Yes, m'lady? How may I serve?

                    MOM (V.O.)   ◄── *Voice over used with filtered*
                (filtered)  ◄────── *parenthetical when over the phone*
            Just checking on you, sweetie. Are
            you doing okay?

                    JONAH
            No worries, m'lady. 'Tis a fine
            day.
```

```
INT. APARTMENT - KITCHEN - DAY
```

Jonah's MOM, dressed in overalls, is underneath a dark and dirty sink as she fixes a leaky pipe. Her phone illuminates the shadowy cabinet. She puts him on speaker.

>                     MOM
>           Well, I'm still fixing Mrs.
>           Johnson's sink. It's going to be a
>           while. How is Sir Gawain?

INTERCUT - MOM/JONAH ← *Intercutting between Mom and Jonah allows the scene to switch between their locations*

>                     JONAH
>           All is well, m'lady. He fights for
>           the light. Today he has encountered
>           the evil Baron Von Naughty and a
>           vicious dragon.

>                     MOM
>           Oh my! He'd better be careful on
>           his adventure. He could end up
>           hurt.

>                     JONAH
>                 (drops the act)
>           Mom, it's just a toy. It's not
>           real, you know.

>                     MOM
>           I... I know son. I just want to
>           make sure --

>                     JONAH
>           I'm staying out of trouble, Mom.
>           Don't worry. No more adventures.

>                     MOM
>           Thank you, sweetie. I love you.

>                     JONAH
>           Love you, too.

EXT. JONAH'S PICNIC TABLE - DAY ← *The Intercut is finished as the scene returns back to Jonah*

Jonah hangs up his phone. Sadness fills him. In the f.g. the toy knight of Sir Gawain stands in a hero pose on the table.

**INSERT:** This is used when you want to have something come into focus and fill the screen. It should be used sparingly and reserved for special moments needed for dramatic effect to further the story. Such as, a love note, ransom letter, a blood-stained weapon, et cetera.

*Side note*: As an alternative, use an action line to describe the Insert instead of using the camera direction. Inserts are becoming passé and less used in screenplays. Below are two ways to use an Insert with and without the camera direction.

With an Insert:

```
The sound of SWORDS CLASHING rings through the air. This is
Jonah's ringtone. He whips out his cell phone.

INSERT - JONAH'S CELL PHONE ←— Jonah's phone fills the camera frame

On it is an image of Lady Guinevere. The screen reads "Mom."

BACK TO SCENE ←— Returns to the previous scene

His eyes narrow with caution as a picture of Lady Guinevere
blinks on the phone. The screen reads "Mom."
```

Without an Insert:

```
The sound of SWORDS CLASHING rings through the air. This is
Jonah's ringtone. He whips out his cell phone.

His eyes narrow with caution as an image of Lady Guinevere
blinks on the phone. The screen reads "Mom."

Jonah answers the phone.    *Descriptive action can make the scene
                             more dynamic without camera direction
```

**b.g. & f.g:** Used as camera directions for when something happens in the background or foreground. Do not overuse these as they will become distracting.

```
EXT. JONAH'S PICNIC TABLE - DAY

Jonah hangs up his phone. Sadness fills him. In the f.g. the
toy knight of Sir Gawain stands in a hero pose on the table.
```
*Camera direction*
```
It catches Jonah's eye.

Frustrated, Jonah picks up the small toy knight. After a
moment, determination crosses Jonah's face. He gently places
the toy back onto the table.

                    JONAH
          No more adventures... but a quest
          awaits.
```

**Ellipses ...** This denotes a moment of dialogue when the character trails off or pauses. Make sure to include a space after the three dots.

**Em Dash — or --** A long hyphen or double hyphen used as an interruption to dialogue. It brings attention to what follows next.

```
                    JONAH
               (drops the act)
          Mom, it's just a toy. It's not
          real, you know.
```
*Ellipses as she trails off before regaining her composure*
```
                    MOM
          I... I know son. I just want to
          make sure --
```
*Em Dash as she is interrupted by Jonah*
```
                    JONAH
          I'm staying out of trouble, Mom.
          Don't worry. No more adventures.
```

**Cut To:** This is a transition to switch to a new scene. DO NOT USE THIS. No one in the industry uses Cut To anymore. Instead, leave these for the shooting script. The script you write will be a reading script and will have no use for this camera direction.

**Cont'd:** Used at a page break, when a character's dialogue continues from a previous page. Or when their dialogue is broken in-between action lines. This has fallen out of style recently and is viewed as redundant. Do not use these in your scripts.

*Protip: Too many camera directions can be distracting and pulls a reader out of the script. Only use a few of them. If your script is filled with b.g./f.g/inserts or the dreaded Cut To, then rework them into your script via descriptive action instead. For example, on the previous page, instead of using "in the f.g." it could read as:

```
EXT. JONAH'S PICNIC TABLE - DAY

Jonah hangs up his phone. Sadness fills him. Jonah notices
the toy knight as it stands tall in a hero pose.

Frustrated, Jonah picks up the small toy knight. After a
moment, determination crosses Jonah's face. He gently places
the toy back onto the table.          *No camera direction
                    JONAH
          No more adventures... but a quest
          awaits.
```

With the description on the previous page, it is implied that the toy knight is in the foreground. This is cleaner, more descriptive, and pleasing to the eye.

## Series of Shots vs. Montage

These two are often confused with one another. Some believe they are interchangeable. That is not true. They each have their own use and purpose in a screenplay.

**Series of Shots:** This is a sequence of quick cuts which shows action being taken by a character. There is no emotion to this scene. It is merely a way to show a fast succession of events. It is also the "gearing up" scene found in most action films such as when Batman throws on his cape, cowl, utility belt, and tries on his gloves.

SERIES OF SHOTS - JONAH GETS READY ← *Add a brief description of the shots*

-- Jonah packs his snacks into a dented red lunch pail.

-- Jonah slings a backpack over his shoulder.

-- Jonah zips up his hoodie.

-- Jonah slides on frayed fingerless gloves and makes a fist.

-- Jonah pulls a hood over his head.


END SERIES OF SHOTS

Jonah stands tall and mighty in the same hero pose as his Sir Gawain on the table. The sun breaks over the apartment building. Its yellow rays cast down behind him.

**Montage:** This is similar in execution to a series of shots but different in context. A montage is a sequence of events which have an emotional quality to them. This is the opening scene in *UP* when Carl falls in love with his childhood sweetheart, they grow old together, and she passes away leaving him in torment. It is often used as the "falling in love" moment in most dramedies and romcoms.

## Subtext

Subtext is the screenwriter's secret weapon. It is what allows us to weave an engaging and immersive depth to a conversation between characters. Subtext is what's behind a character's dialogue. It is their hidden intent, a veiled expression from one character to another. It is the true meaning behind what is said.

In *Jurassic Park*, John Hammond often says "Spare no expense." However, if you look at how unfinished the park is, that it is run by a skeleton crew, and equipment frequently breaks down, you realize that he actually cuts corners wherever and whenever he can.[65]

In *The Empire Strikes Back,* there is a great moment of subtext between Lando and Darth Vader after Han and Leia are captured on Cloud City. Lando tells Vader "You said they'd be left in the city under my supervision." To which Vader

---

[65] Jurassic Park. Directed by Steven Spielberg. Universal Pictures. 1993.

replies, "I am altering the deal. Pray I don't alter it any further."[66]

The subtext to the scene is palpable. Should Lando cross him then he will be at Vader's mercy. Had this been a direct a conversation it would be far less intriguing. The subtext makes the scene powerful and ultimately an iconic moment in the Star Wars saga.

```
INTERCUT - MOM/JONAH

                    JONAH
          All is well, m'lady. He fights for
          the light. Today he has encountered
          the evil Baron Von Naughty and a
          vicious dragon.

                    MOM
          Oh my! He'd better be careful on
          his adventure. He could end up
          hurt.
                    JONAH
              (drops the act)
          Mom, it's just a toy. It's not
          real, you know.
```

*The subtext implies she is concerned for Jonah and not his toy knight*

---

[66] Star Wars: Episode V – The Empire Strikes Back. Directed by Irvin Kershner. 1980.

## Visual Subtext

Remember, screenwriting is a visual medium done in the written form. This means we are not limited to only using dialogue as subtext. With screenwriting, we have the privilege to use the medium by painting subtle visual cues throughout our story. This allows us to deliver visuals and glimpses of our characters' inner emotional struggles directly to the audience's subconscious. They won't even know it's there. They will just know there was something about that scene or moment in the script that they really liked.

```
Jonah faces the oppressive building. He stands tall and
mighty in the same hero pose as his toy knight on the table
beside him. Majestically, the sun breaks over the apartment
and shines upon Jonah.
```

The above segment clearly paints a picture of Jonah accepting his role in the story. He is ready for this adventure as he proudly stands in the same hero pose as his toy knight. The above visual subtext is created to be a dramatic moment for this sickly little boy. However, visual subtext can be very subtle to the point where it's easy to miss.

Take the film *Passengers* for instance. This film is about a man on a colonization ship crossing the stars on a 120-year journey. A man on a pilgrimage, Jim, is accidentally awoken from cryogenic suspension early on in the trip. Unable to return to his long sleep he is doomed to spend the rest of his life alone. Stuck and desperate, he awakens Aurora from her cryogenic pod knowing that she can never be put back asleep, damning her to be stuck with him. After a series of poor judgments, Jim realizes just how terrible a person he is. There is a scene which stands out. Jim enters his bedroom to change his clothes. He opens the closet to find it empty. At first, this scene seems random. Until you realize the closet represents Jim's inner struggle. It is empty because he feels empty. He is hollow inside. [67]

Looking to dive even further into formatting?

Then check out David Trottier's *The Screenwriters Bible* or *The Hollywood Standard* by Christopher Riley.

---

[67] Passengers. Directed by Morten Tyldum. Columbia Pictures. 2016.

## Formatting Tips

- Avoid using camera directions. Instead, cleverly hide them in your action.

- Ease up on the parentheticals .

- Leave out the scene numbers .

- Get rid of the widow words from your descriptive action. That is a word left alone on its own line of action.

- Make your format flawless.

- Action blocks should be four lines or less.

- Write like a spartan. Use fewer but more powerful words.

- Leave plenty of white on the page.

- Do not add cast lists or cast descriptions.

- Introduce speaking characters. Only capitalize them the first time.

- Do not describe your characters based only on their appearances. It is assumed they are attractive. If they are not and it is part of the character, then add that to the description

- Grammar matters. Make it perfect.

# PART IV: WHAT COMES NEXT

You've written a screenplay! Congratulations! You have now done more than most people and have joined the fellowship of screenwriters. You're not done though. Now it's time to truly lean in, protect this script and make it perfect.

## WGA Registration vs. Copyright

Registering a script with the WGA will mark a script as an original work by you but that does not safe guard it from plagiarism or from being stolen outright. The only way to truly protect a script is by copyrighting it. This ensures the screenplay will have legal protection by the US government. In a lawsuit, if you only register with the WGA, then you have to pay legal fees even if you win. This can result in long, drawn-out legal cases which can destroy you financially. With the US Copyright, if the case rules in your favor, then the fees are waived, and you get a settlement for infringement. A WGA registration cannot do that. Copyrighting a script can be a longer more tedious process, but it is worth it.

*Side Note*: A concept alone can **NOT** be copyrighted. This is why there are numerous films with strikingly similar concepts. The difference between them is the interpretation and execution of that concept into a finished screenplay. That is what can be copyrighted.

## Rewrites

Never show anyone your first draft. Ever! I know you're excited but trust me on this. First drafts are terrible and riddled with problems. You need to do at least a dozen drafts. Yes, a dozen. Then you need to ship your script off to be polished. Either by a brutally honest friend, "Grammar Nerd," or a professional service. Either way, you want a clean script to send out.

## Coverage/Notes

I would recommend you send out that clean script to a professional service for notes, aka "coverage," and to three peers as well. You need a professional opinion: they are in the industry and know what works, but you must ensure they are reputable. As a professional screenwriter and consultant, I am often brought in to fix the work of bad "Script Doctors." You need to know what you are getting into. Remember your script is entirely unique. Just as you are. There is nothing else out there identical to it. Are there similarities to others? Of course. But it is yours and it is special. Why would you trust it with just anyone? That's why you must be careful.

If you are getting a "deal" from a service, there's a reason for that and it usually means they are shady. Also, check their IMDb credits. Do they have any work that's been produced? Are they actively working in the industry? Can't find them on IMDb or they don't list the names of their

Script Doctors? These are big red flags. Check word of mouth as well, reputation means everything in this business.

Many Script Doctors are writers or producers who weren't able to make it in the industry and turned to script doctoring as a side gig, yet these sites will charge exorbitant amounts of money. It's a scam. You'll find a lot of those. These sites also tend to give overwhelmingly negative feedback in hopes of coercing you into a more expensive service that would help you magically improve your script. Don't fall for it. Work with people who want to see you succeed. Not with someone who views you as their next meal ticket.

**Feedback**

Feedback hurts. It sucks. As writers, we rip open our chests and bleed onto our work. We infuse ourselves into it. Thus, any kind of criticism we receive can feel like a gut punch to the soul. As much as that hurts though, in the end, it doesn't matter. You know what does matter? The work. Your script. You have to do whatever it takes to make your screenplay killer.

Thus above, you will send your script to three peers you trust. You must be judicious about who you choose. Never use a friend or family who is overly supportive. Their notes will be polite, complimentary, and completely useless. You need notes from someone who isn't afraid to be brutal. That is the sign of a true friend. Someone who will tear it apart, and be unafraid to use words such as derivative or cliché.

Once you receive notes from your peers, break them down, look for similarities. Are there common threads or comments about certain sections of the script? If so, they are issues that must be addressed in a rewrite.

Never be defensive or justify your decisions. There is no quicker sign of an amateur than someone who cannot handle criticism. Remember a professional wants notes. We crave them. Because we want the best script possible for our producers/managers/agents, so they have something truly remarkable to work with.

*Side Note*: If significant changes are made to the script during the rewrite process then it should be reregistered with US Copyright.

## Synopsis

A synopsis is a summary of the script. It broadly focuses on the most important moments of your story.

**Short Synopsis**: This is longer than a logline. It is one full paragraph to one half-page long.

**Full Synopsis aka the One Sheet:** This is a full breakdown of your script.

*Side note*: Some synopses can run as long as three pages if acceptable to the producer. In general stick with the One Sheet.

# Guide for a Synopsis

Use the main story outline to arrange your synopsis:

1. Introduce the character
2. Inciting Incident
3. Plot Point 1
4. Pinch Point 1
5. Midpoint: Death and Rebirth
6. Pinch Point 2
7. Plot Point 2
8. Resurrection
9. The Return

Now plug the outline into the template on the following page.

## Synopsis Template

**Screenplay Title** – Make sure it is capitalized
**Genre** of your script
**Logline** – Keep it under two sentences

## Synopsis

The first few paragraphs will cover act one. It will include an introduction of the Central Character, the inciting incident, & plot point 1.

The midbody of the synopsis will encompass the Act II beats. This is the bulk of the synopsis. It covers pinch 1, the midpoint, pinch 2 and plot point 2

The last few paragraphs of the synopsis cover the resurrection and return of the Central Character.

Your name
Phone number (address is not necessary)
Email

## Treatment

A treatment is a breakdown of your story written in prose. There is no set template for a treatment as they vary from writer to writer. Some can be as long as 40 pages. On average a treatment is six to ten pages. When writing a treatment follow the same format as the synopsis but build it into six pages at approximately two pages per act of your screenplay. Make sure to include your logline and a brief breakdown of major characters.

A nice example of a treatment is available online via creativescreenwriting.com. Simon Kinberg shared his treatment for the hit action film *Mr. & Mrs. Smith*[68], and it's free to download.

When requested to turn in a treatment to a producer, ask them the style of treatment they prefer. How many pages do they want? Do they have a favorite treatment? This will give you a heads up on how to best meet their expectations.

## The Query

This is a way to pitch your script to people in the industry via email. Essentially you are cold-calling talent managers/literary agents/producers/even actors. It is viewed as junk mail.

It is extraordinarily difficult to reach success in this way. Although it can happen, it is rare. For

---

[68] Simon Kinberg, Treatment for *Mr. & Mrs. Smith* courtesy of creativescreenwriting.com 2001

example, I didn't receive a credible response from a producer until I had sent out almost a thousand queries. At one point I even used a query service to improve my chances. Eventually, my zombie comedy garnered some attention and actually made it all the way to Fred Siebert, the founder of Frederator. They make television shows for Cartoon Network, such as the *Fairly Odd Parents, The Powerpuff Girls,* and *Adventure Time.* Fred was so impressed with my script, he sent it down the line to his VP of development. Who requested to read more of my work. Though this did happen, it is a rarity. It is the 1% chance, a fluke of nature.

Although I garnered a modicum of success from it, I want to be very clear. I do not recommend writing queries. They tend to go nowhere. I agree with the former film executive of MGM Pictures, Stephanie Palmer in her article *The Great Query Letter Hoax* in which she states, "In rare instances, a query letter will get the attention of a legitimate decision-maker. But this is a very low-percentage event. Actors have been discovered waiting in line at Starbucks. That doesn't mean aspiring thespians should get coffee over and over again all day long."[69]

There is a better way to find success and that is through networking, which will be covered in the next section.

---

[69] Stephanie Palmer, *The Great Query Letter Hoax* courtesy of goodinaroom.com 2015

## Agents vs. Managers

Landing representation is what every writer wants. Some writers believe if they can land an agent then it will make their career. Those desperate writers will lose their minds and their pocketbook by trying to find an agent by attending pitch fests (which are usually scams) or querying everyone under the sun. I should know – I've done both.

### Agents

The truth is an agent won't waste their time on you unless you are a produced writer of a film which has done moderately well or has something of a buzz around it from some of the higher-profile festivals. Then all of a sudden they will pop up out of the woodwork. Agents will approach you. Once signed, an agent will ship your work out to studios or even produce it themselves under their own production company. They will be more focused on whichever project you have at the time. An agent will take a 10% commission fee.

### Managers

A manager is far different. They tend to have a smaller stable of writers than an agent. Thus you get more attention from them. A good manager will want to build up your career and do what they can to help you in general. There are managers who even help their writers land acting gigs if that is a career their writer is focused on as well. That won't happen with an agent. It's far easier to get a manager. With positivity and persistence, you can get through the door with one. It helps if you are able to build up a reputation within the indie community through winning awards at festivals or end up having your script produced.

A great way to look at a manager is that they are the key to a door. A manager will use connections to query producers and studios for you. Whereas your queries were ignored before, when sent by a manager, your queries will actually be read and not automatically thrown into the junk mail folder. A manager will take a 15% commission.

Protip: Never pay a manager up front. They make their money on the sale of your script. If a manager asks you for any money up front, such as a retainer fee, then they are a fraud. Managers are not regulated by law as an agent is. Thus the field can be littered with scammers.

# PART V: NETWORKING

Once the script is finished and you have gathered the essential materials, it is time to put yourself out there. As much as we love to be hermits and hole up in our comfy writing nooks, we need to get out there.

## Branding

To be successful, we have to stand out from the crowd. Calling ourselves a screenwriter and trying to land gigs on our own will not work. We need to be something more. That's where a brand comes in. We live in a branding society. Everything has a brand from the laptop I'm using, to the drink I just spilled on it.

Branding will help you stand out from the pack. Without it, you are a ghost and lost in the shuffle of over 100,000 people who call themselves screenwriters.

First and foremost, it's essential to build a website. It's the first step to being found. However, it has to have meaning. There needs to be a niche or need that you can fill with your skill.

Had my website said GeoffreyDCalhoun.com I would have never had a client nor made a name for myself. Most screenwriters try to brand themselves by name. Unless you're already a huge name in the business, it doesn't work. At best it comes off as vain. At worst we disappear into a sea of online lost souls.

Figure out who you are and what you excel at, then build a brand around it. As wefixyourscript.com it is obvious exactly what we do and how we do it. The name itself already carries weight. Now answer the following. What do you offer as a screenwriter? How can you make that unique online?

## Building your online presence

This is so important in today's society. Are you Googleable? As a screenwriter, if we are not the entire first page online when our name is searched, then we don't exist. That's a problem. How can you stand out from the crowd if people can't find you?

Let's start with the basics needed to build an online presence.

- Facebook
- Twitter
- Instagram

You need to post on these at a regular pace that you can handle. For some people that's four times a day per platform; for others, it's far less. To avoid posting-fatigue try using Buffer or Hootsuite. These will allow you to post to all your social media at once or even schedule them for a future date.

Create bios on these sites:

- LinkedIn

  - Write compelling blogs on your profile. They populate when you're searched and give a great first impression

- Mandy.com

  - You can post a resume which can be seen by producers who visit the site

- ISA (International Screenwriting Association)

  - Use the "My Successes" option on their website. It allows you to enter any awards you've won which will show up when you are googled. It's like guilt-free bragging

- IMDb (Internet Movie Database)

  - An IMDb profile will be the first thing that pops up when you are searched. You will be right at the top. I mean come on, that's just cool

All of these are a must. The SEO (search engine optimization) on these sites is astounding. Creating complete bios will give you a huge boost to your online presence. After doing this myself, I became the entire first page on Google.

Winning awards also allows you to see where you stand with your peers. Are you first place? Second place? A finalist? Why? Find out what is working and what is holding you back so you can continue to succeed and improve your work.

Blogging is essential. Getting a strong following for your blog is difficult. However, it will increase your SEO on your website if you blog regularly. Also, guest blogging is a must. If you can guest post on blogs which are already established with a following, then all the better. Every little thing you do will add to your online street cred and quickly build your reputation.

## Online Networking

We are in the digital age. You'd be surprised what kind of connections you can foster online. Once you have thoroughly branded yourself and have a digital footprint, then you can really get out there and make waves online. You will need to post on, and from relationships on:

- Stage 32
- LinkedIn
- Facebook writers' groups
- Twitter
- Reddit
- Quora
- Mandy.com

All of these sites are great places to network online. They allow users to interact with other writers, producers, and directors. You'd be surprised who you can meet to forge ahead with your own coalition.

## Tips on Networking

- LinkedIn: Become an all-star status by making connections and writing blogs. This makes you more prominent on the site and can lead to great opportunities if you actively engage with people you connect with

- Meetup.com: A great place to join a local writer's group

- Find talent at local film festivals for future collaboration

- ISA: Has meetups online Wednesdays and every third Thursday at different venues around the world. I've been lucky enough to be a guest speaker at one in Toronto. It was a blast!

- Facebook: There are countless writers' groups just waiting for you on this platform and they are free!!!

## Awards

You don't have to win at the top ten film festivals to be successful, but you do need to take the script you've written and get it out there. Make sure you enter contests within film festivals which have large attendances that will provide ample opportunity to network.

Being an award-winning writer at a festival carries weight when pitching your work to others. It gives you a degree of prominence and sets you apart because your work has been weighed, measured, and found worthy. Of course, the better known the festival, the more impressive your wins.

## Film Festivals

Networking is your greatest asset to success as a screenwriter, bar none. It is what will provide you with more work and help get your name recognized among filmmakers. Film Festivals are a must for any serious writer and an excellent place to meet people at various stages of their careers.

Some festivals allow you to pitch to studios, walk away with cash prizes, an internship at a network, see your script optioned, or even get a contract with a Hollywood talent manager/agent.

At the very least, a fest may offer "lateral networking" which is still worthwhile. It allows writers to band together, which can lead to future collaborations.

## Full Script – *A Mighty Quest*

Attached is the full script of the award-winning short screenplay *A Mighty Quest*, which was used as samples in the formatting section of this book. While reading it, see if you can spot the nine-point main plot outline, the heart plot, the supporting character plot, and the Antagonist's plot.

A MIGHTY QUEST

By

Geoffrey D. Calhoun

info@wefixyourscript.com
601-885-3491

FADE IN:


EXT. APARTMENT BUILDING COURTYARD - DAY

The tall, brick apartment building reaches high into the sky
like a medieval tower.

JONAH, a sweet 10-year-old boy, sits alone at a weathered
picnic table.


EXT. PICNIC TABLE BATTLEFIELD - DAY

A great toy battle has been fought on this table.

There's a greasy ogre tipped over on it's side, a set of
dominoes stacked like an ivory staircase, and a tiny, beat-u
plastic action figure of SIR GAWAIN, a brave knight in gray
armor, who stands tall and proud.

                    JONAH (O.S.)
                (as Sir Gawain)
        Let her go, Baron Von Naughty.

Across from Sir Gawain is the evil BARON VON NAUGHTY, a
plastic action figure of a classic wizard. At his side, boun
by twine, is the PRINCESS, a Barbie doll whose hair has been
burned off.

                    JONAH (O.S.)
                (As Baron Von Naughty)
        No. She is mine. Ahahahaha --


EXT. JONAH - DAY

COUGH COUGH. Jonah pulls out an inhaler. He presses it to hi
mouth and clicks the button. He inhales deep.

After a moment, his coughs cease. His eyes catch...


EXT. DAISY'S WINDOW - DAY

DAISY, an adorable yet pale blonde 10-year-old girl who
watches him play from her window high up in the building.

He smiles to her and waves. Daisy waves back. He beckons for
her to come down and join him. She shakes her head no.

EXT. JONAH - DAY

Jonah sadly nods as he bites into a peanut butter and jelly sandwich. He tucks that away and then pulls out a chocolate chip cookie.

                    JONAH
              (As Baron Von Naughty)
          I can stop you with my magic!

A crunch is heard as Jonah takes a bite of his cookie.


EXT. PICNIC TABLE BATTLEFIELD - DAY

The knight stands tall as a few cookie crumbs, which appear like boulders, crash down nearby with earth-shattering BOOMS.

                    JONAH (O.S.)
              (as Sir Gawain)
          Your magic cannot stop me.

                    JONAH (O.S.)
              (as Baron Von Naughty)
          You think you have won?

BOOM BOOM CRASH -- enter a giant, black dragon toy.

                    JONAH (O.S.)
              (As the princess)
          Oh no, a dragon!


EXT. JONAH - DAY

Jonah looks up and sees Daisy is gone. Only an empty and open window remains.

                    JONAH (O.S.)
              (as Sir Gawain)
          Fear not, princess. I will free you
          and smite this foul --

The sound of SWORDS CLASHING rings through the air. This is Jonah's ringtone. He whips out his cell phone.

His eyes narrow with caution as a picture of Lady Guinevere blinks on the phone. The screen reads "Mom."

Jonah answers the phone.

                    JONAH
          Yes, m'lady? How may I serve?

                    MOM (V.O.)
               (filtered)
          Just checking on you, sweetie. Are
          you doing okay?

                    JONAH
          No worries, m'lady. 'Tis a fine
          day.


INT. APARTMENT - KITCHEN - DAY

Jonah's MOM, dressed in overalls, is underneath a dark and
dirty sink as she fixes a leaky pipe. Her phone illuminates
the shadowy cabinet. She puts him on speaker.

                    MOM
          Well, I'm still fixing Mrs.
          Johnson's sink. It's going to be a
          while. How is Sir Gawain?


INTERCUT - MOM/JONAH

                    JONAH
          All is well, m'lady. He fights for
          the light. Today he has encountered
          the evil Baron Von Naughty and a
          vicious dragon.

                    MOM
          Oh my! He'd better be careful on
          his adventure. He could end up
          hurt.

                    JONAH
               (drops the act)
          Mom, it's just a toy. It's not
          real, you know.

                    MOM
          I... I know son. I just want to
          make sure --

                    JONAH
          I'm staying out of trouble, Mom.
          Don't worry. No more adventures.

                    MOM
          Thank you, sweetie. I love you.

                    JONAH
          Love you, too.

EXT. PICNIC TABLE - DAY

Jonah hangs up his phone. Sadness fills him. In the f.g. the toy knight of Sir Gawain stands in a hero pose on the table.

It catches Jonah's eye.

Frustrated, Jonah picks up the small toy knight. After a moment, determination crosses Jonah's face. He gently places the toy back onto the table.

> JONAH
> No more adventures... but a quest awaits.

SERIES OF SHOTS - JONAH GETS READY

-- Jonah packs his snacks into a dented red lunch pail.

-- Jonah slings a backpack over his shoulder.

-- Jonah zips up his hoodie.

-- Jonah slides on frayed fingerless gloves and makes a fist.

-- Jonah pulls a hood over his head.

END SERIES OF SHOTS

Jonah faces the oppressive building. He stands tall and mighty in the same hero pose as his toy knight on the table beside him. Majestically, the sun breaks over the apartment and shines upon Jonah.

INT. APARTMENT BUILDING LOBBY - DAY

Jonah enters the old lobby. The walls are damaged and the tile floors are cracked. There is hardly anyone there.

The building MANAGER, a tall and massive Neanderthal-looking fellow in his 50s, naps behind the front counter.

FRONT COUNTER

Jonah sneakily walks around the corner and creeps up to him.

A large ring of keys hang from the Manager's hip.

Jonah looks about left and right. No one can see him. With deft hands, Jonah grabs the keys and gives them a tug.

The Manager squirms for a moment. His hand falls onto Jonah'
face. The manager's hand twitches, mid-dream.

Jonah's eyes grow large as one the Manager's fingers brushes
up against Jonah's nose.

Jonah snags the keys and quietly sneaks away. The keys rustl
in his hands.


INT. APARTMENT BUILDING LOBBY - DAY

Jonah walks up to the elevator. A sign reads "Out of order".

He turns and looks to a massive staircase. His shoulders
slump with defeat.

                    JONAH
          The dreaded Staircase of Woes.


STAIRCASE

Jonah is near the top of the stairs when the manager enters
at the bottom of them. The Manager looks up and sees Jonah
with his keys.

                    MANAGER
          Hey, kid!

Jonah pauses, mid-step.

                    MANAGER
          Give me those keys.

Jonah runs for it. The Manager gives chase.

Jonah runs up multiple flights of stairs as the manager
follows like a lumbering giant. Each step he takes makes the
ground shake.

He tries to grab Jonah, but he's too quick and light-footed.

Jonah dances around people on the stairs as the manager
shoves them out of the way.

Jonah is almost to the top until he catches a stitch in his
lungs. He can't breathe. The Manager lumbers towards him.

Desperate, Jonah swings his lunch box. The old tin box hits
the Manager's stomach. The ogre of a man laughs it off. Jona
pulls out his inhaler.

e Manager grabs his set of keys from Jonah's hand. Jonah
ruggles, but loses the fight.

>          MANAGER
>          (chuckles)
>     Take your medicine, kid.

nah looks at his bottle. It reads "1" charge left. He
esses it up to his mouth, pauses, then pulls it out before
ing it.

>          JONAH
>          (wheezes)
>     Wait.

e Manager leans down.

>          MANAGER
>          (sarcastic)
>     What? Need me to call your momma
>     again?

nah reaches up and sprays him in the eyes with his inhaler.

e Manager screams and drops the keys. He falls to his knees
d holds his eyes.

nah can't breathe. His eyes flutter and his head spins.

T. HOSPITAL - DAY - FLASHBACK

nah lays in a hospital bed, pale and weak, with an oxygen
sk over his face. His PARENTS are behind a curtain with a
CTOR, washed out by a white light.

>          MOTHER (O.S.)
>     What are you saying?

>          DOCTOR (O.S.)
>     He needs to be careful. Too much
>     exertion will take its toll. He got
>     lucky this time.

T. APARTMENT STAIRCASE - PRESENT DAY

e manager catches his breath.

>          MANAGER
>     Why did you do that, kid?

                    JONAH
              (coughs and wheezes)
          I'm on a mighty quest.
              (calms his breathing)
          I... I am Sir Jonah.

He slowly rises.

                    JONAH
          I must free the princess.

He grabs the keys and his lunch box. With a renewed vigor, he
stands tall.


HALLWAY

Jonah gets to a door that reads "The Von Knotts" Jonah tries
different keys. None of them work.

The manager is at the other end of the hallway. His eyes are
teary as he squints and rubs them. His vision is blurry.

                    MANAGER
          Where are you?!

Jonah tries a few more keys. The manager's eyesight improves

He looks around, but no one is there.


INT. DAISY'S APARTMENT - FAMILY ROOM - DAY

Jonah quietly locks the door. On a nearby couch stirs Daisy's
father BARRY, a grease monkey in his late 30s. Still asleep,
Barry rolls over to reveal a silly logo of a car and taco on
his shirt which reads "Barry's Autos and Tacos."

Jonah snickers at the logo then quickly hides behind a chair

Jonah crawls towards Daisy's room. He comes to a stop when a
large, black dog greets him with a growl. From its thick neck
hangs a name tag that reads "Drake".

                    JONAH
              (fearful)
          The Black Dragon.

Drake slowly pushes towards Jonah; its jowls full of slobber
The mutts beady eyes stare him down as if he's a fresh dinner
to be devoured.

Jonah slowly crawls backwards until his back hits a wall.

                                                    104

                        JONAH
            Uhhh... good boy?

Drake growls and shows its teeth. Jonah's asthma returns. He
can't breathe. Jonah grabs his inhaler. It has "0" charges.

The dog leans in. They are face-to-face now. Slobber drips
onto Jonah. Drake is about to attack when... FART! Drake
looks over as Barry, still asleep, rolls over on the couch.

Panicked, Jonah looks to Daisy's room. Her door has a sign
with her name on it sparkled in glitter. Jonah closes his
eyes and finds his inner strength.

Jonah calms his breathing. Color returns to his face. Jonah
POPS open his tin lunch box. Drake turns back with intensity.
Jonah pulls out his secret weapon: half a peanut butter and
jelly sandwich.

                        JONAH
            I smite thee, foul beast.

The dog's head turns with curiosity. His tail wags, excited.
Jonah tosses the sandwich. The dog chases after it. Jonah
rushes towards Daisy's room.


DAISY'S ROOM

Jonah quickly enters the small princess themed room.

                        JONAH
            M'lady, it is I, Sir Jonah, here to
            free...

He is shocked to find Daisy on her bed. Daisy smiles when she
sees him but is embarrassed. She is sickly, pale, and bald.
She has oxygen tubing wrapped under her nose.

Daisy grabs a blonde wig that rests on a mannequin head
nearby and puts it. She quickly looks away in shame.

QUICK FLASH - JONAH AND DAISY MEET IN THE HOSPITAL

-- Jonah is pushed in a wheelchair by his mother. Jonah sadly
contemplates the inhaler in his hand.

-- Daisy passes Jonah as she walks with her father. She
appears healthy.

-- Jonah turns around, as does Daisy. They lock eyes. Jonah
smiles to her. Daisy shyly smiles back and waves.

BACK TO SCENE

Jonah notices how upset Daisy is. He sits down on the bed
next to her. He gently reaches out to her face. She shies
away. He delicately removes her wig and sets it aside.

Daisy, still embarrassed, bravely looks over to Jonah. He is
there with love in his eyes and a big smile. She lets out the
breath she had held in this whole time.

INT. DAISY'S APARTMENT FAMILY ROOM - LATER

Barry wakes up on the couch. He sees Drake constantly lick
his lips in the corner of the room. The window is open.

Children's laughter outside catches his attention. He looks
out the window where he sees...

EXT. JONAH'S PICNIC TABLE - DAY

Daisy and Jonah are shoulder to shoulder with their backs to
her father. Daisy has her oxygen tank with her. Its plastic
tube runs to her nose.

Daisy and Jonah happily giggle as they play with Jonah's
toys. Jonah opens up his lunch box and offers her a bite of
his cookie.

She takes a big bite and they both giggle. Daisy reaches over
and places her hand on his open palm. He tightens his grip
around hers.

The sun passes through clouds and shines on them both.

                                          FADE OUT.

*A Mighty Quest* – **Analyzed**


**Concept:** A sickly little boy believes he is a knight of the round table.

**Theme:** There is strength in all of us even when we are at our sickest. (Wo)Man vs. Them Self

**Main Character:** Jonah

**Supporting Characters:** Mom, Daisy, Jonah being irresponsible.

**Logline:** A sickly young boy convinced he is a knight embarks on a quest to free a princess from an apartment building at great risk to his health.

**Main Plot:** Jonah must free Daisy.

**Subplot I – Heart Plot:** Jonah's Mom is worried about him. He is concerned about Daisy.

**Subplot II – Supporting Character:** Jonah's Recklessness and irresponsibility are the supporting subplots. With a short story and micro-shorts, it can be more compelling to combine plots into a single character.

**Subplot III – The Antagonist:** The real villain of this story is not the Building Manager or Drake, the dog it is Jonah's asthma itself. That is the true battle he must fight.

## *A Mighty Quest:* **9 Point Main Plot Outline**

1. **Inciting Incident:** Jonah notices Daisy as she sits sad and alone trapped in her room.

2. **The Debate:** Jonah is warned about the ramifications of adventuring by his mom.

3. **Plot Point I:** Jonah stands tall as the sun shines down on him. He accepts his quest.

4. **Pinch I:** Jonah sneakily steals the keys from the Manager. The chase is on as Jonah tries to make his escape up the staircase.

5. **Midpoint – Death & Return:** Jonah suffers from an asthma attack and suddenly collapses.

6. **Pinch II:** Flashback to Jonah being hospitalized from his asthma. His attacks can be fatal.

7. **Plot Point II:** Jonah Encounters Drake. The dog threatens to tear Jonah apart.

8. **Resurrection:** Jonah gathers his inner strength and confronts the dog with a mighty weapon. His trusty PB & J sandwich.

9. **Return:** Jonah and Daisy sit together at the picnic table. Jonah shares a cookie with her.

## Subplot I: **The Heart Plot**

1. **The Debate:** Jonah's Mom warns him to be careful and stop having his adventures. Jonah begrudgingly agrees until he realizes he must take on this mighty quest to save a princess.

2. **Midpoint - Death & Rebirth:** Jonah's asthma gets the best of him. He has a flashback of him in the hospital where his worried mother is told about how dangerous his asthma is. Jonah will not be defined by it.

3. **Plot Point II:** Breathless and with no charges left on his inhaler, Jonah finds the strength to continue by seeing Daisy's name written in glitter. He must free her. She's counting on him!

4. **Return:** Jonah finds Daisy and realizes how sick she is. He has a flashback of seeing her in the hospital where they first met. He frees her from her external prison as he has released himself from his internal prison as well.

## Subplot II: **The Supporting Character Plot**

1.  **Plot Point I:** Jonah's mom is scared and worried about her son. His reckless adventures put his life at risk. Jonah doesn't take her seriously.

2.  **Pinch II:** A flashback shows the results of Jonah's behavior. He has been hospitalized and is barely able to breathe.

3.  **The Return:** Jonah finally realizes the toll disease can truly have on someone. Jonah frees Daisy but now carries the responsibility that decision comes with. Daisy has on her oxygen while they are at the picnic table.

## Subplot III – **The Antagonist plot**

1.  **The Inciting:** Jonah is playing with his toys and has a coughing fit. He must take a puff from his inhaler.

2.  **Midpoint – Death & Return:** Jonah not only overexerts himself but he collapses as well. His asthma has taken its toll. He may not survive.

3.  **Resurrection:** With his medicine gone and a terrifying dog baring down on him. Jonah finds the will to continue.

## In Conclusion

The intention of this book is to be a compendium of the great screenwriters and their influencers. Those who have elevated our craft and brought their knowledge to the next generation of screenwriters. I hope you found something in this book that has sparked a thought or idea about screenwriting which pushes you to learn more. If so, then I have done my job and have passed the torch once again. Below is the list of books used as inspiration for this text. I hope you find yourself diving into them as I did when I began this journey over a decade ago.

# Bibliography

Campbell, J (1961)
**The Hero with a Thousand Faces**
Mumbai, India - Yogi Impressions LLP

Campbell, J (1990)
**The Hero's Journey**
Mumbai, India - Yogi Impressions LLP

Vogler, C (1998)
**The Writer's Journey: Mythic Structure for Writers**
Studio City, CA – Michael Wiese Productions

Mckee, R (1997)
**Story: Substance, Structure, Style, and the Principles of Screenwriting**
New York, NY - Harper Collins

Field, S (1984)
**Screenplay**
New York, NY – Bantam Dell

Field, S (2008)
**The Screenwriter's Workbook**
New York, NY – Bantam Dell

Snyder, B (2005)
**Save the Cat**
Studio City, CA – Michael Wiese Productions

Tierno, M (2002)
**Aristotle's Poetics for Screenwriters**
New York, NY - Hatchette Books

Trottier, D (1994)
**The Screenwriter's Bible: A Complete Guide to Writing, Formatting, and Selling Your Script.**
Los Angeles, CA – Silman James Press

Riley, C (2009)
**The Hollywood Standard: The Complete and Authoritative Guide to Script Format and Style.**
Studio City, CA – Michael Wiese Productions

Additional Texts

Gladwell, M (2008)
**Outliers: The Story of Success**
Little, Brown and Company

Leman, K (2015)
**The Birth Order Book**
Grand Rapids, Mi – Baker Publishing Group

Stephanie Palmer,
**The Great Query Letter Hoax**
goodinaroom.com 2015

## **Acknowledgments**

I want to thank all of those who have supported me during this crazy career. My mentors: Del Weston whose insight and wisdom have guided me to heights I never thought possible. To Richard Brandes whose knowledge of filmmaking and screenwriting is incalculable to my success. To my friend and fellow literary survivor Amanda Arista who allows me to pick her brain clean at the oddest times of day. To my editor and wordsmith Jayne Southern and to everyone who has believed in me and indulged this wild dream of mine. Thank you from the bottom of my heart.

*Photo by CKJR - Charles Kennedy Jr.*

## About the Author

Geoffrey D. Calhoun is a Top 100 Indie Screenwriter and Founder of *WeFixYourScript.com*. Aside from his own screenplays, he is known as a script doctor and consultant for films. He is also director of the *Script Summit Screenplay Contest* which is listed as a Top 20 Biggest Contest by The Script Lab.

Made in the USA
Middletown, DE
25 May 2019